MY BROTHER WAS MY KEEPER

MY BROTHER WAS MY KEEPER

VADA ALLEN- JOHNSON

XULON PRESS

Xulon Press
2301 Lucien Way #415
Maitland, FL 32751
407.339.4217
www.xulonpress.com

Unless otherwise indicated, Scripture quotations taken from the King
James Version (KJV) – *public domain.*

Paperback ISBN-13: 978-1-6628-0844-9

Ebook ISBN-13: 978-1-6628-0845-6

Table of Contents

Now would be a perfect time to introduce you to one of the greatest influencers in my life and the reason for my survival, my grandfather. Truth was utterly important to my grandfather and he had the most confounding way of presenting his truths and ideas. It has taken me decades to unravel some of his truisms and each time one unravels, it brings to mind a vivid memory usually accompanied by a chuckle. The following conversation took place between my grandfather and my five-year-old self. I hope you enjoy it.

Me: "Papa, why does telling the truth get some people in trouble sometimes?"

Papa: "Oh, because most likely they started out telling a lie, then when they could not remember all the lies, the truth had to come out. By then everybody's mad at somebody or somebody is mad at everybody."

Me: "So, it's not just kids that lie?"

Papa: "No, Baby. Grown folks lie too and they're better at it."

Me: "Then Papa, when will people learn telling the truth is better than lying?"

Papa: "When chickens crow."

Me: "You mean when roosters crow, Papa."

Papa: "No, Baby. No, I don't. Some folks will only tell the truth when chickens crow."

Me: "I don't understand Papa, chickens don't crow. Only roosters crow."

Papa: That's right, Baby. When chickens crow, people will always tell the truth."

My Papa insisted on living within the confines of truth no matter the cost to yourself or others; in the end, the value received would be worth the cost.

Within these pages and until I no longer have the urge to write, my life and my truth will be on display. I have endeavored to use few true names because by doing so I would demand a defense by others. I give no one the right to defend their actions in my life. They did what they did and I will not allow them or those who loved them the space or time in my life to change or excuse what has happened.

From the time of my birth and until very recently, I have had to apologize to one person or another simply because I existed. No longer. This is my absolute, unapologetic telling of MY life, as I lived it, as it was demanded of me to live it.

Many of the un-named people of whom I will write about are deceased. Perhaps, the timing of this writing was divinely inspired to allow the ones who thought themselves virtuous, (who refused to admit to the damage done to me by their actions), time to make their exit. Regardless of the lies they told me, others, and themselves, and in spite of the reasons they sought to break me, they're gone, and yet I live to tell my truth!

The Chickens are crowing, Papa!!!! The Chickens are crowing!!!

Three men played undeniably outstanding roles in my life. These three men laid the foundation for everything I would need to know to transverse the landmine filled roads that had been laid before me. These three men taught me self-knowledge and self-awareness, yet understanding the differences between the two, took years to fully grasp. These three men showed me love by their reflections, two positively, one negatively. Two of these men taught me that denying self was needed to fully achieve love and in denying self, the love that was poured out upon others, would be returned in immeasurable ways. The other man taught me that self-centeredness only feeds the ego and offers nothing beyond self-gratification and gives nothing of kindness to others. Two of these men became the lamp-light which pushed back encroaching darkness, the third man was darkness.

In one way or another, each of these three men had a hand in shaping my life and I am grateful to each of them. There need not be great imagination or supposition to understand how one can learn and grow from the bestowing of love and kindness, but much can be gained even from darkness. These three men, I loved all three, two deserved my love one did not yet I cannot help but remember the words of 1 Corinthians 13:

If I speak in the tongues of men or of angels, but do not have love, I am only a resounding gong or a clanging cymbal. If I have the gift of prophecy and can fathom all mysteries and all knowl-edge, and if I have a faith that can move mountains, but do not have love, I am nothing. If I give all I possess to the poor and give over my body to hardship that I may boast, but do not have love, I gain nothing. Love is patient, love is kind. It does not envy, it does not boast, it is not proud. It does not dishonor others, it is not self-seeking, it is not easily angered, it keeps no record of wrongs. Love does not delight in evil but rejoices with the truth. It always protects, always trusts, always hopes, always perseveres. Love never fails. But where there are prophecies, they will cease; where there are tongues, they will be stilled; where there is knowledge, it will pass away. For we know in part and we prophesy in part, but when completeness comes, what is in part disappears. When I was a child, I talked like a child, I thought like a child, I reasoned like a child. When I became a man, I put the ways of childhood behind me. For now we see only a reflection as in a mirror; then we shall see face to face. Now I know in part; then I shall know fully, even as I am fully known. And now these three remain: faith, hope and love. But the greatest of these is love.

THE THREE MEN

"Call Me Mister!"

Papa	My Grandfather	Robert Allen
Chinee	My Brother	J.B. Allen
Mister	My Father	G.W. Lewis

This chapter, centered around my birth, will perhaps be the most difficult to write. Difficult because to tell my story, I will likely and sadly, be putting my mother in a position to again be judged by people who do not know her story. I am telling no more of her story than what is needed to tell mine. I will say that as a young mother of a newborn baby, she waded through a decade when judgment of her as an unmarried mother, created turmoil and captured the unwanted attention of some in our community. She captured the attention of some who filled their free time sitting and gossiping over telephone party-lines instead of standing and whispering over backyard fences. Those who spend their free time making pariahs of those they considered cheap and not worth their time, unless that time was spent engaging in acts which actually cheapened them in their sad indefensible attempt to feel superior by disparaging others. I will not honor them by naming them, but we knew them, oh yes, we knew them.

In life, my mother chose to walk with her head held high. She walked above the trash that was purposefully strewn at her feet. She admitted to her mistakes and asked forgiveness from the only one who mattered, her Lord and Savior. Her solid belief in God allowed her the ability to walk between the stones hurled her way by those, I supposed, who thought themselves without sin.

That early pain to which I had been subjected, had been precipitated by promises my father made and broke to two women; one of whom my birth so infuriated that she attempted, (and almost succeeded) to remove me from her life, permanently. Although it was decades before I told anyone of her attack, the fact that I did not speak of her attempt right away, only served to embolden her hatred of me.

The other never learned of this attempt on my life and died without knowing. However, the one who desired my demise feared my exposure of her until the day she died.

My conception and birth had been whispered about, snickered about, made sport of, and blatantly discussed at times in front of me. I was the recipient of unearned pain caused gleefully, it seemed to me, by some uncaring and unfeeling adults. It was from them I learned that I was a pitiful little girl, that I was an unwanted pox upon their community. They also taught me that I was a bastard; a word I did not understand but sensed by their tone that I should be ashamed at being. Contrary to what might have been a normal reaction to their hateful taunting, I'm grateful, for they unwittingly taught me the meaning of," Do unto others as YOU WOULD HAVE THEM DO UNTO YOU." They also taught me to be inclusive, without meaning to.

My father's Friday night ritual was to visit my mother and me. I was unapologetically a daddy's girl and I anticipated those visits with unbridled delight (I was five) even though my mother no longer did. I can't be sure how often, but my father certainly used many of those visits to not only provide some financial support and a bag of treats for me, but to also plead his case for another opportunity to be allowed back into Mother's life. After Mother had finally made it clear to my Father that he would not be allowed back into her life and that his visits would only be tolerated for the sake of his and my relationship, both the visits and the financial support begin to wane.

My purpose here is not to lay blame on the bed of my parents. Everyone makes mistakes and, once acknowledged, should be offered the opportunity to move on without the constant reminders and recriminations to which my Mother was subjected. Although I am a product of their mistake, I AM NOT a mistake! I am here however to take issue with how my birth was handled by my father and one of those two women, a mistake of which I cannot, nor will I forget.

I did not understand why my father no longer came to visit me as he had most of those first five years of my life yet even so, all was not lost. My father attended the same community church as my family which meant I would see him on Sundays!

My father had attended church with some regularity because he held a position of prominence within the church. Dad owned several businesses one being a small mobile resale business which presented itself well in a community lacking any type of nearby general store or market, therefore he benefited from making a few extra dollars selling to a ready-made crowd, after church; true early ingenuity.

Even though I had suffered disappointments because of my father's diminished visits, I had yet to feel the sting of rejection but when I did, it happened in a most public and painful way.

It happened one Sunday afternoon after church services. All the little children from my Sunday School class ran outside and gathered around Dad's truck, jockeying to be first in line to spend their nickels. This was the first time since Dad had discontinued his visits to me that I dared to approach his familiar green truck. I had been prevented from doing so on previous

Sundays by a sister five years my senior. This time however, I had run ahead of her because she had been delayed inside the church.

By the time I reached the front of the line, there were only teenagers and adults standing behind me who were also waiting their turn to purchase treats. I stood there expectantly waiting for the same hug Dad had given the other little girls prior to exchanging their nickels for treats but no hug came to me. With disappointment ripping through my little soul, I tried holding back tears. Failing miserably, I next tried to manage what I later came to know as rejection, by softly asking for a bag of M&Ms, my favorite candy. However, instead of Dad reaching into his truck and coming out with that beloved brown bag of colorful chocolate morsels, which would have gone great lengths toward healing my very recently injured heart, he stared down at me from his several inches over six-foot height and demanded the nickel from me that I did not have. It never occurred to me that my Dad would exact payment from me for a nickel bag of candy but then I never supposed he would withhold a hug from me either.

My humiliation was complete as he, too loudly, told me to run along, to come back only if I had the price of the M&Ms and to never expect something for nothing. I had heard nothing funny in what he said but apparently, everyone waiting behind me had been let in on a joke. A joke at my expense. What really broke my heart was hearing Dad's familiar laughter mingling with everyone else's. I could not have felt more shame. Although, I really loved M&Ms, all I had really wanted was the hug that Dad no longer brought to me on Friday nights.

Since I was only five, I could not decide if the lingering pain I felt came from *not* getting those M&Ms, not getting the hug, or maybe it was because he had shooed me away while laughing at me. I do remember thinking as I walked away, that one day when I grew up, I would have all the M&M's I could eat and would not have to ask him for any of them. I could not have known then that over 40 years later and 1800 miles away, I would be employed by a division of Mar's International. The very company which created and produces trillions of colorful little tidbits called M&Ms...who, as a benefit of employment, sat boxes of them on a display rack just inches from my desk and I never had to pay for a single bag or ask anyone for them. By the time I left that company, the only things that I missed from my childhood and had not reconciled, were hugs from my father...

The chickens are crowing, Papa.

Mother was not unaware of the swirls of gossip that centered around her in our community. At one point, it had become so ubiquitous that it forced her to refrain from attending our local church. The church of which both my maternal and paternal grandmothers were instrumental in establishing. It was for this reason, among others, that led to a life changing conversation. Thinking back, I can correctly surmise that the age of five had been a monumental juncture in my life. Perhaps that is the reason most of my memories from that period are so vivid. With eyes closed, one of those memories rushes back demanding critical reflection.

I can clearly hear Mother's voice calling me inside from early morning play. As I ran in, she motioned me forward and we sat at our kitchen table. I can see that big, ancient, well-seasoned, beautiful round oak table sitting squarely in the middle of our kitchen. Throughout many decades, that table had held service for countless, humble but delicious family meals. Many lifetimes of tears, some shed from happiness but legions more from grief and longing stained its untreated surface; it had served as a desk and warm place to complete hundreds of hours of assigned homework for children and for doing piecework for my grandmother's lovely quilts. However, perhaps best it of all, it had provided tired and weary bodies a welcoming place to catch a breath and reflect. It was there, at this achingly familiar fixture, where Mother picked me up and sat me on her lap. I remember catching a subtle whiff of her special scent which consisted partially of Long-Aid hair dressing, (the pink jar), Camay soap, and Jergens lotion. Those fragrances mingled with the unique smell of the fairly new oilcloth covering our table. Dinner, already simmering on the stove, also lent its mouth-watering aroma to the cacophony of odors coming together in unison almost as if to cover the stench of fear that would soon give rise in that kitchen.

Oh, how I wish I could remember what was simmering in Mother's pot that day, how it tasted, whether I had eaten that evening's meal, or if I had gone to bed without dinner as I sometimes did when some fear or fright caused my stomach to clench. I have no memory of those wished for things. Where in my memory did they go and why am I unable to grasp and hold unto them? Those lovely things I would much prefer to remember but they will not come to me, however the frightful ones come unbidden. Maybe the fear Mother's words caused me erased those things I now wish to recall. Her words, her warnings, meant only to protect me, had the effect of a door closing upon my childhood and a slow spiraling away from that which was familiar and so sadly fleeting. The ache of a childhood which was pulled away too soon had no ready salve or poultice to soothe that painful extraction.

On that morning as we sat there, I remember nuzzling my face against Mother's neck and inhaling another comfortable fragrance. A fragrance of which I still associate only with her. The fragrance was Avon's Topaz Cologne, a sweet, spicy scent which she had earlier delicately dapped in the hollow of her neck. It invited me to lean in closer and just as I was about to totally give in to the comfort I felt leaning there against her breast, childishly enjoying this rare moment of bonding, she asked me what turned out to be a most worrisome question. She asked if I knew a particular woman whom she named. Admittedly, at my tender age, my circle of family, friends, and acquaintances was not extensive, but because of the size of our community, its people were well known to each other. Unsure whether I should say anything I instead kept my head down, nodded, and waited for her to speak again. As I waited, I somehow sensed she was about to say something that was going to change my life and not in a good way.

"Aunt Sally" was one of my mother's love names for me, one which in my estimation, she only used when something bad was about to happen; "Just close your eyes, Aunt Sally," she would say while she too frequently extracting splinters from my errant fingers. "Open wider, Aunt Sally," while pulling a loose but stubborn tooth. When telling me that it bothered her more than it bothered me as she was forcing Castor oil down my throat at the beginning of both winter and spring; "Swallow it, Aunt Sally, it'll be easier if you swallow quickly." At the clinic in town, "Don't cry, be a big girl. Aunt Sally," as I was getting drilled by a needle as long as an Épée and likely just as painful! Always, always something bad followed, "Aunt Sally." This time was no exception.

"Aunt Sally, if you ever see this woman anywhere and I'm not with you, stay away from her," she said. Her words did not sound as light as I believe she wanted them. I nodded again, this time frightened by the anxiety and desperation she tried to prevent but could not keep from finding a home in her voice. "Do you understand?" she asked, Her voice now hard-edged and tight with tension, yet even so, she allowed her soft right hand to gently cup my chin as she lifted my face upward, my eyes then meeting hers. "I won't always be with you baby, so you need to learn now which things and people to stay away from." This conversation and warning took place during a time when children lived purposeful yet carefree lives, especially in farming communities. During a time when they had no worry of "Stranger Danger" as long as they stayed within the confines of their communities. Because within the confines of those communities, children where looked after, loved, and protected by all the adults. It was that whole "it takes a village to raise a child" thing. Well, that highly regarded adage applied to everyone it seemed, except my family. In a community of similarly, economically situated families, an unspoken caste system was nevertheless established and because of telephone party-line judgments, we were at the bottom.

My whole, albeit immature & incomplete, understanding of the adults around me had begun to shift. Having only recently learned that adults lie, I was now being told I would have to somehow protect myself from one of those adults and that left me without the necessary vocabulary to express what I was feeling. Whatever it was I had felt in that moment, elicited such a strong emotion it was as though I had inwardly grown an additional appendage, useful only to create fear effectively performing what it was created to do.

During those interminable moments, Mother sought to prepare me not only for a world where not all adults could be trusted but also a frighteningly nightmarish world in which she would not always occupy. I remembered her words and the warning she issued that morning...until I did not.

The woman of whom Mother issued a warning was the second woman to whom Dad had broken promises. I suppose in some miserly, empathetic way, I can allow myself to envision and understand the weightiness of her position; however, the weight of her perhaps legitimate complaint did not belong on my tiny shoulders.

It takes no great pain to assert that I have no personal knowledge of any discussions which might have taken place within the home my Father shared with this woman. Further, if I knew, I could not divulge it here because again, it would not be my story to tell and having never been invited into his home, I could have laid no witness to anything that might have occurred there. But conversations about me assuredly happened there. The fact that they are both long deceased does not hinder or soften the affect their lives and the decisions they made had upon mine and it is that affect, of which I apply unchallenged relevance. I understand that some, who have known of me and the others of whom my story involves, could possibly have reasons to contemplate my truthfulness in this matter however, as I've said from the beginning, my truth is my truth, and no one's opinion challenging my truth matters. No one suffered or carried these scars except me. I make no apologies.

The woman hated my existence. I suppose because I was a constant, breathing reminder of my father's infidelity. She was the woman who shared not only his home, but his life and should have been the woman to whom he was faithful alas, he was not. Their relationship and her hatred of me notwithstanding, *I am his daughter.*

As I contemplated the sharing of this next chapter of my life, I imagined people I know, who are still living or perhaps even those both long ago and recently departed, would likely have advised me, "to let sleeping dogs lie". Meaning, to leave things as they are, to avoid restarting or rekindling an old grudge, or to leave old disagreements in the past; but I don't intend to do either of those things because those dogs are lying on my bed! Beyond that, as long as I live, as long as my children live, and as long as their children and the ones following them live, I will teach them to fight for their places in this world. This painful rendering of my life will prayerfully encourage them to never remain silent when their right to exist is challenged. The quiet path I was made to travel, now yells loudly that silence is not always golden.

Mother never again mentioned the warning she had given me months before, and I had not forgotten, not yet. This was the early '60s and a time of change, a shifting of old notions was happening. A new decade bringing new promises and it seemed everyone was excited about the possibilities of changes in the political arena and new hope ran rampant. Everyone I knew was letting go of the past and straining to reach toward a new future just beyond their reach but near enough to keep grasping for it. Everyone, as it were, except one.

It was the summer of my sixth year, and I was too soon to be heading to first grade. My second eldest sister and her husband came visiting from their home in California. During their visit, my brother-in-law treated me as though I was his own special princess placed in his life to be constantly fawned over by him alone. The fact that I was a child favored with neither loveliness or even a pixie cuteness and having been deprived of my father's attention, caused me to glow under his welcomed attentiveness. Each time he left the farm and returned during this visit, he would present to me with great flair, a package of my beloved M&M's! Any cavities I developed later in life could undoubtedly be traced back to this fleeting, "almost" idyllic summer. Oh, how I loved this man; he was everything I imagined a man should be. If there was an adult hero in my life at this time, other than my grandfather, my brother-in-law filled the bill that summer. He was tall, terrifically good-looking, strikingly strong, and he had a smile that could melt solid chocolate into a smooth silky stream in seconds. Kindness exuded from him yet there seemed to be just under the surface, a tautness, a readiness to spring into action to defend anyone he loved. I felt safe and protected with him; he was also my first crush. He knew the special place he held in my life and he tolerated my quiet, constant adoration in such a deliberately sweet way that for years as I approached early adulthood, every male in my life was measured by my brother-in-law.

It was during this visit on one especially brilliantly beautiful East Texas mornings and just a few days before my sister and brother-in-law were scheduled to return to their West Coast home, he'd thought to surprise my younger sister and me with a day at a park near our home. It was a popular place which offered not only a green area for children to play, but also a fairly long dock reaching out into a large, lovely, blue lake (though it was called a pond). It was here that fishermen spent long hours angling, visiting, and sharing cold beers hidden openly in coolers which traveled in the trunks of cars or in the passenger section of their pickup trucks. Unbelievable thoughtfulness was even afforded to the women of the area by offering them a Washeteria, aka Laundromat on the property so that they might keep busy with laundry duties as the men enjoyed their leisure. This laundromat was located out of view and beyond earshot of the dock. It was also several steps below ground, I suppose to somehow help cool the large non air-conditioned room.

Before we arrived at the park, my brother-in-law stopped for snacks: sodas, chips, candy, and a brand-new red rubber ball for me! It was a rare treat to receive a new toy at any time other than Christmas. I was enthralled. It was turning into an incredibly special and memorable day indeed. I would later recall that day not so much from the joy it brought, but for what marred that joyful, brilliantly beautiful East Texas summer day.

As my brother-in-law and sister pulled fishing poles from the car's trunk, I was given strict but gentle instructions to stay away from the water's edge. I was to stay within their eyesight as I played with my ball. This seemed fair enough. We agreed to it and off we went.

I played on the paved area of the parking lot, bouncing, and tossing my ball into the air. I was thrilled when I caught it and chased after it when I missed. One of my misses sent me chasing my new ball across the parking lot. It bounced & rolled faster than I could catch up to it and I watched as it rolled down the steps into the laundromat, out of sight and earshot of my family.

Momentarily uncertain, I looked around quickly and just as quickly decided to chase my ball down those steps; with my eyes down, I searched for and spotted the ball as it rolled across the slick linoleum floor. I ran toward it and just as I caught up to it and reached down to pick it up, a foot covered it. I mistakenly thought that foot meant to prevent my ball from rolling further. I was grateful for the help because I wanted to escape this dimly lit room and return to the parking lot before I was missed.

I tugged at the ball, but the foot would not relent. I could not comprehend why the foot would not remove itself from my ball. Desperately desiring an answer as to why the foot stayed instead of releasing the ball, I looked up and met a face that sent cold, consummate fear throughout my small body and gripped my heart with a pounding force not even adults should suffer. It was far beyond what a not quite six-year-old child should suffer. The new ball now forgotten, as the face of my mother's warning loomed above me. Time slowed. Actually, time seemed to go backwards as colorful snapshots of me sitting on my mother's lap at our kitchen table flickered across my mind's eye. Memories of mother's soft hands lifting my chin were far removed from what was happening now. I was now looking into the face of my nightmares! My nightmares had become reality as she forcefully lifted and turned me so that my back was pressed against her abdomen. I squirmed trying to get away, seeing the door but unable to move toward it, because her desire to restrain me was every bit as urgent as was my desire to get away. My fear was no match for her hatred, and I was losing this battle. I felt a painful, tightening sensation around my neck that made screaming impossible. The pressure increased and I felt as it would cause my head to explode. The dimly lit room was getting darker and I could hear mother's voice calling my name. Calling, calling, calling...but I could not answer because the darkness had stolen both my voice and my sight. My last conscious sensation was feeling the confusingly cold yet warm floor beneath me. That confusing situation was then made caustically clear in my fading thoughts...the cool linoleum floor was being introduced to the warm contents of my bladder as the nylon stocking she wrapped around my neck grew tighter and still mother's voice called to me from somewhere much too far away.

I have no idea how long I laid there alone in a dim corner of that laundromat but just as I had heard mother's voice calling to me as I was forced into unconsciousness. I was again hearing my name being called and it roused me from the dark place I had been cruelly sent both carnally and spiritually. Even so, the sound of my name being called had an edge of panic attached to it. That sound frightened me almost as much as opening my eyes and perhaps seeing that dreaded, hate filled face above me again. When keeping my eyes closed began to frighten me more than opening them, I forced my grit filled and swollen eyes opened and saw nothing above me except an overflowing sink spilling water onto the floor, soaking my urine-stained dress. I was grateful for what was surely a purposeful flooding because it masked the shame of my soiled dress. Twice now within only a few months, adults had caused me humiliation beyond imagination and this one almost cost me my life. I wish I could say that the physical and emotional abuse I suffered from adults ended here but this was sadly, only the beginning.

The voices calling my name came from my sister & brother-in-law. They sounded closer than they had when my eyes were closed. *They were looking for me! How long had I been away*

13

from their sight? I attempted to stand but each time I tried the room would spin, defeated, I sat down on the water and urine-soaked floor and begin to tremble at the thought of mother discovering I had been disobedient by not heeding her warning. All my fears converged and caused tears to join the water and urine, soaking me thoroughly. I squeezed my eyes shut again wanting, this time, to surround myself in darkness; too afraid of seeing the bad things that showed themselves in the light.

As my younger sister entered the building, I heard her say, "I looked in here already," to which my brother-in-law responded, "There's water running in here someplace, did you see water on the floor before?" My sister answered, "No." As their footsteps drew nearer, my panic would not be contained, and shock engulfed me. Still afraid to open my eyes, I felt myself being lifted again but this time by strong, caring arms; arms that were safe and comforting not clawing and choking. Even so, my brother-in-law alternately uttered soothing and berating words. Soothing while trying to stop my violent shaking and berating because of the fear I had caused him by not staying where he had told me to stay. He must have finally noticed that the shaking of my body had nothing to do with the cold water I had been lying in and he hugged me closer, protectively to his taut, angry, though not at me, strong chest.

I cried without making a sound, my swollen eyes were no longer capable of producing tears. As I was carried outside, I dared a peek and saw that the bright blue sky that had been when I'd chased my ball into the laundromat, was now changing into the orange, gold, and purple hues of a Texas sunset. I had been unconscious and hidden from view for hours.

Freed from the dungeon that was to have been my temporary tomb, my brother-in-law tried handing me the red ball he had purchased for me a lifetime ago. Instead of grasping it, I shrank from it, no longer wanting it because now, in my mind, there would always be a disembodied monstrous foot attached to it. He carried me to his blue sedan and placed me in the huge back seat. He told me how he and my sister had searched for me, even looking around the fringe of the huge pond afraid I had fallen in. He asked me where I had been and how I had come to be in that laundromat after they had previously searched it? I had no memory of leaving the laundromat until he carried me out. With the shaking somewhat abated, I attempted to answer his questions but try as I might, the words that formed in my thoughts could not be released by my throat. My vocal cords had been damaged by the stocking that had been tightened around my throat. Finally, a good omen...not being able to talk saved me from having to tell mother that I had forgotten what she had told me to remember!

This all happened around the week of July 4, 1960. Whether the assault happened before or after the holiday, I am no longer sure. It was however about six weeks or so before the start of school, but now even two weeks after the assault, my voice had still not recovered, despite the abundance of cold ice and warm teas I had been forced to consume. I had no idea when the swelling of my vocal cords had subsided or that my voice had returned until the day my mother escorted me to school on my first day, which was many weeks after everyone else had started school. After she had deposited me into the care of my first-grade teacher and as she turned to walk away, a fear closely akin to what I had experienced more than 3 months before was unleashed as I screamed to mother and pleaded with her not to leave me alone. I'm not sure which of us was more startled at the months-long unheard sound of my hoarse crackling voice but she turned back to me, leaned down, and with tears in her eyes, she kissed the top of my head and whispered, "Be good and listen to your teacher, Aunt Sally."

The chickens are crowing, Papa. NOT THE ROOSTERS! Decades later, with tears afresh, I'm screaming, "THE *CHICKENS ARE CROWING, PAPA!*"

By that fall of 1960, Mother and Papa had ceased from questioning me about the incident at the park's laundromat and the consequences of it. Their questions had stopped but not their suspicions. I'd overheard my grandfather, whispering to mother one evening that unless she wanted him to handle the problem, his way, she had better handle it and soon. My Papa's manner of handling things was with a bandolier of birdshot shells and a 12-gauge shotgun. He was sincerely invested in the "live and let live" philosophy of life as long as the sentiment was honored by all concerned; if it wasn't, the offending party would likely spend the better part of several days getting profoundly familiar with a pair of tweezers and a bottle of Mercurochrome, that is to say, if they were lucky.

Mother told her dad, my Papa, that she would talk to "him". Hearing her assurance given to Papa, did nothing to reassure me that the laundromat subject had finally been dropped. I had thought, innocently, that as long as I said nothing about that woman and if she said nothing, certainly Mother would never have to learn of our shared sick secret. I had never knowingly been exposed to deliberate adult deception and this time I could not climb onto Papa's knee or go for long walks with him across the farm, asking him of this most daunting question without telling him why I was asking. The idea of lying to Papa was not something I could imagine. "*Papa*" was a synonym for "*Truth*" and those two words could not be separated in my mind. So, although my voice had returned, what had not was the sense of security which had once covered me. While I felt some measure of security on the farm, it would be decades before I would be able to let my guard down completely around any female. On more than one occasion, my cautiousness proved a valuable asset.

Now, it was seldom, if ever, that I would ask Mother to allow me to accompany her on one of her rare trips into town. I felt safer staying near Papa and his ever-ready, ever-loaded, double barreled shotgun than I felt with Mother and her small, at the bottom of her purse, five-shot .22 pistol. The Monster of my nightmares, whose movements, clunking around barefoot and rattling chains, was not limited to the under-bed area of innocent children's bedrooms. My Monster was not one who disappeared when the sun rose and shone light into dark corners. My Monster's life consisted of visiting laundromats and strangling little girls. No, Mother's little .22 wouldn't work on my Monster! I'd been witness to the type of damage that the little pistol could do. It would make a tiny hole upon entry and unless it hit a vital organ or nicked an artery, the recipient of such a hit could still exact a measure of damage of its own before succumbing. No, much better to stay with Papa, whose shotgun, when both barrels were deployed, could lift a 10-point buck off its feet while buckshot spread throughout its body, simultaneously hitting multiple organs at once. Not so wonderful for a deer but that type of firepower was exactly what was needed to put down a Monster who wore sensible, black, lace up women oxfords, printed cotton housedresses, and who smelled faintly of Oxydol detergent, Clorox, and sweat.

My resolve never to leave the farm again except for school and church was broken one Saturday morning not long after I had overheard/eavesdropped on Mother and Papa's conversation. After which, seeing one of my five school dresses laid neatly across my bed, did not inspire hope for indulging in one of my favorite Saturday morning pastimes, trailing Papa around the farm. There would be no Mighty Mouse, no Top Cat, no Jetsons, or Flintstones cartoons.... I recall standing there and glancing sideways at a multicolored polka dot dress as if it might sit up on its own accord and speak to me. Although one of my favorite dresses to wear, I preferred to wear it only during school days! Saturdays were not meant for colorful polka dot dresses, ruffled nylon socks, or black patent leather Mary Janes anymore!

Before I could mount an efficient protest, Mother had slipped the dress almost magically over my already freshly braided slicked back hair and we were walking outside and climbing into the waiting open door of a car being driven by Mother's friend. Sitting alone in that big back seat, I finally had a really good reason to stay home. A reason not even the prospect of a promised store-bought treat was enough to squelch. The grumbling of my too sensitive stomach and the blinding headache beginning to form behind my eyes would have been my reason, had they had happened just ten minutes sooner. My now almost constant headaches had become all too familiar after the Laundromat. My incredible short life had been divided into two areas of time: "before" the Laundromat and "after" the Laundromat. I had learned early on not to complain about the headaches because to do so brought on the dreaded questions. It was lost on no one that the headaches appeared on the same day my voice disappeared.

The car made several stops after we reached town. There were quick stops at Syler's Rexall Drug Store and Harrell Meats and Bean's Grocery Store before the car entered a street off the main boulevard and near enough to Nick's Café that I could smell grilled hamburgers, onions, and coffee punctuating the late morning air. I remember stifling a laugh as we passed by R&R Electric Company, who by using the plug end of an electrical cord, created their cartoon character mascot. Not yet encountering any monsters in the daylight had eased both the discomfort in my stomach and the throbbing in my head. The three of us were now just sitting in the car without conversation. No explanation was offered to me as to why we were now just sitting there. I tried to make sense as to why I was sitting here in this backseat instead of my sister who would have been infinitely more helpful to Mother if she would by chance need someone to help her do whatever she'd mistakenly brought me along to do. Why were we just sitting? I did not dare ask and subject myself to "The Look." My frustrations would not allow me to sit still, no matter how many times Mother told me to stop fidgeting.

Just as I was about to risk life and limb by speaking of my frustrations to Mother, I noticed her motioning to her friend to look across the street. I followed their glances and saw a familiar dark green pickup truck parking at the end of the street and unfolding out of it was my Dad. Why was he here? Was he the reason we had been sitting here waiting? The headache that had ridden with and abandoned me the first half of the trip had suddenly returned.

Flashbacks to a day I wanted to forget were returning side by side with the headache. My mind was super-imposing Dad's face over that woman's face! Although he had not been in the laundromat that day, in my mind, he and she were undeniably linked, for better or worse, for richer or poorer, until death did *I* part. Mother exited the front of the car; told her friend she wouldn't be long, while opening the back door and beckoning me to slide out. I did not want to. Mother took my hand in hers and began to close the distance between us and Dad. He did nothing to help shorten the distance and simply continued to lean against his truck. Mother half pulled, half dragged me behind her, and I had to run on tippy-toes to keep up with her. As the renewed pounding in my head increased, the realization that I had also never told Mother of my last encounter with my father, who before that fateful Sunday afternoon, I had lovingly called Daddy, made me nauseous. The day I had last heard his laughter when he had punctured by heart from behind me. The thought of just how many secrets I was hiding from Mother became almost too much for me to contain and I groaned aloud. Mother slowed only momentarily to make certain that my overly sensitive stomach was not releasing its contents on my dress or on the town's pristine street. Once satisfied, the march toward the end of the street continued. I wanted to go home; I wanted my Papa. Maybe Mother knew that I had not been telling her the truth! Maybe she no longer wanted me! *Maybe, maybe she was going to send me to live with my Dad and the Monster who lived with him! Maybe it wasn't too late to tell her about everything. Maybe, if she knew she would not send me away to live with them!* My mind was so busy sorting out my options that I had not noticed that my father had finally left his truck and was making movements toward us. With no longer any need to close the distance, Mother's abrupt stop caused me to bump into her.

From seemingly nowhere, Mother's friend appeared, and handed mother the purse that always held her .22. The friend took me by the hand and crossed the street with me in tow. Although I was happy not to have to look into father's face, I nevertheless did not understand why I could not have simply stayed in the car in the first place! Even though we were across the narrow street and several shop doors away from Mother and my father, I heard their voices rise. I saw my father towering over Mother, and she stood defiantly in the midst of his anger with her hand resting inside her opened purse. Dad's voice suddenly quieted as Mother yelled, "TELL HER!" Tell who what, I wondered. "YOU TELL HER!!!" Mother said again. My father looking down but not at mother seemed defeated. "But before you tell her, let me tell you this: if I ever find proof that either of you have touched her or hurt her in anyway, neither Humphreys, his deputies, or the threat of a jail will keep me from sending both of you to hell!"

My heart dropped...I knew who the "Her" was...Me! And I knew now that she was indeed sending me away with a warning to them! I'm positive neither of those three adults in attendance there that afternoon was aware that I *was* aware of them. The very recent past however, had taught me to be vigilant regarding my surrounding. Sadly, I was learning to pay closer attention to how adults spoke and what their faces said when they spoke and less to what they actually said. Reading adults, I later learned, is something at which some physically abused children become quite proficient. I was one of those "some."

Mother's words held dual meanings as she purposefully modulated those two singular syllabic and threatening words, "Tell Her." The first "Tell Her" is what quieted and stilled Dad's voice. The seconds "Tell Her" made Dad glance in my direction. I held Mother's friend's hand tighter...was Dad coming to tell me that he was taking me with him? Would I have a choice? I wanted so badly to go to my **dark place**; the place where I had learned to go when things became too difficult for me to ponder my way through. The place I would go when the Fear would come. Mother's friend obviously felt my hand going slack inside of hers. In that moment, I no longer needed the comfort her hand had supplied. I felt myself drifting toward the place where everything went away. All monsters, all fear, all cynical laughter, everything simply receded, and quietness would take over. Darkness and quietness held hands which meant I no longer needed to. I was free to "Be."

As I grew older and lost the ability to go to my dark place, I searched for places just to "Be." I was never quite as successful at finding a "To Be" place as I had been at finding my dark place. Wanting "to be" became a familiar refrain for me and those close to me recognized my need "to be." To be left alone. To be quiet. To be irresponsible. To be happy. To be unaccountable. To be unencumbered of memories that held no smiles.

I am not altogether certain when I lost the ability to go to my dark place but somewhere along the way, I realized that going there left me vulnerable and unable to control my surroundings.

That fateful Saturday afternoon, as my hand slacked in her hand, Mother's friend called my name and said, "You know they love you, don't you?"

"Huh? Who?" I did not know if this question was her first to me or the last in a series. I looked up at her in confusion. "Who loves me?" I asked.

"Your mama and daddy" she answered. With that, suddenly an entirely heretofore unconsidered idea came to me and I allowed myself to consider it! "Maybe Mother and Dad were going to get back together, and we were going to be a FAMILY!" With that thought, a bubble of joy and anticipation flooded over me and for the first time that day, I allowed myself to smile.

Now anxious for Mother and Dad to close the distance that separated us on that quiet back street and have them "Tell Me" their good news. It was as if they had heard my wish because they began to walk toward us. I wanted to run and meet them, but I was prevented from doing so as my mother's friends' hand encircled mine again. I looked at her almost annoyed until I saw a look of concern on her face. I followed the direction in which she was looking and instead of seeing smiling and happy faces accompanying their slowed steps, there were scowls and cold determination. No warmth emanated from either of their faces! Dad's face reminded me of when he had instructed me to never expect something for nothing. And yet I had done just that! Just moments before, having done absolutely nothing to deserve it, I expected Mother and Dad's reunion. What could I have done to prevent this or what did I do to cause all of this? Everything seemed to be about me, but I did not know why. Mother's face looked as it had when she had informed me that I needed to learn whom I could trust. My dark place was a much better place "to be" than standing here in the bright of day, where all of my monsters lived. Bad things did not come to me at night, always they came in the sunshine and they were always dressed as adults!

Now within only a few strides, neither of them reached for me. Mother called to me and I looked at her with pleading eyes to not say or do any hurtful thing. I did not want to look at Dad, honestly afraid of what I would see, afraid of maybe hearing his mocking laughter again.

Mother came to fetch me, and her friend had to pry her hand from my fingers. Mother's hand replaced hers. Whatever was about to happen was not going to be good and was not going to be good for an awfully long time.

Now standing directly in front of my father I sensed there was to be no leaning down to my level, no kiss planted on top of my head, no soothing strokes on my arm. He simply and coldly stood looking down at me. Mother calling me by my familial name said, "Your father has something to tell you, but before he does, I'm going to tell you that I can't prove it because you won't say anything, but I know someone did something to hurt you that day in the washeteria." She did not stop there, "I don't have proof, but I believe I know who did it."

Looking up at Dad's face I saw his temple area throbbing and his jaw was clenched tight. I had seen him angry before but never like this. Mother, not yet finished, continued, "I'm not going to ask you to tell *me*, but I am going to ask if you want to tell *him*?" I shook my head so violently from side to side that several of the barrettes holding my short braids in place flew into the street. "O.K. then," Mother said, "but I've told him what I believe happened and now he has something to tell you." I wanted my father to fold his six-foot three-inch frame down to my not quite four-foot height. I wanted him to take me in his arms and tell me he was sorry for what his personal monster had done to me. I hoped, even without telling him what had happened, that he would promise to never let anything, or anyone hurt me again. I wanted him to tell me that he was going to go to his house, take the monster who lived in his house to Sheriff Humphrey's and let him put her where she belonged. I so wanted my father to be my Daddy again. But he did not come down to my level. He did not tell me he loved me or that he was sorry. He did not pick me up so that I could lie my head on his broad shoulders. He did not calm my fears; he did not offer to kill the monster as she had tried to kill me. He did not offer to let the Sheriff take her away so that all other little girls would be safe. No, he did none of those things. Instead, he asked if I understood who he was. Puzzled, I was thinking there was really something wrong with that question. Of course, I knew who he was, but I knew better than to say what I was thinking aloud, so being both wary and oddly relieved, I nodded. He told me to speak up! "Yes, Sir," I said, offering him the "respectable, well raised, Southern child affirmative." "Then who am I?' He demanded. This was beginning to travel far beyond by mastery of comprehension. I stole a glance at Mother and she almost imperceptibly nodded her approval to answer. Shyly, "Daddy," I answered.

Seemingly, from miles above me, I saw his chest rise as he inhaled deeply. "YOU WILL NEVER CALL ME THAT AGAIN! DO YOU UNDERSTAND?" Crumbling and unable to save myself the embarrassment of crying on a public street, tears flowed. I nodded again completely unable to comprehend why either of my parents would have me endure this new pain. Barely noticeable lines around Mother's lips deepened. Her bottom lip disappeared between her teeth causing her to look as though she wanted to cry as well. I wanted to be as strong as she was and not let this man standing above me see my tears. I only wanted him to see how much I needed him to love me. Where was the man who had sat with me on his lap every Friday night, who shared his dinner with me, who had fed me from the same spoon as we both indulged in our favorite dessert, banana pudding? Where was the Daddy who would gently rock me to sleep as mother washed and put away her pretty deep garnet dishes; the ones she only used to serve Daddy? He did not deserve my tears and I did not deserve the cause of my tears. But what had I done; how could I fix it?

I did not know this man. This man, who had chosen to ridicule me months earlier with derisive laughter. This man who had just seconds ago told me that I could no longer call him "Daddy." I heard Mother almost scream to him, "For God's sake, just TELL HER!" He called my name and I looked up, causing my tears to now run down my cheeks instead of simply dripping to the ground. "Sir?" I choked out. "No matter where you are, if you ever see me anywhere, at Church, in stores, anywhere there are other people, Do Not Ever Call me Dad or Daddy. From this day forward," he said, "*Call me Mister.*"

Hearing those words were every bit as strangling and breathtaking as had been that nylon stocking as it was twisted around my neck; except this time, it was my heart being strangled.

Perplexingly, I never held Mister responsible for the instructions he gave me that day. With insight that belied my years, I realized it was she, the Monster, who demanded he break contact with me. Thirteen or so years later, I would receive validation of that thought. However, I do hold him responsible for the manner in which he'd broken contact. It would have been far kinder to have simply ignored me; to have openly denied my existence. But to have offered me love, shown me love, then to not only take that love from me but demand that I forget it ever existed, was cruel. I have to admit, he taught me a couple of lessons that day I've never forgotten. Trusting anyone completely is a mistake. Believing that love will never hurt is an invitation for constant heartache. Hard lessons for one so young but my Papa taught me early that a "bought lesson is a learned lesson" and I paid dearly for those lessons, never again expecting anything for nothing, indeed, I paid.

Less than 6 years later my Mother at only 44 years of age would be dead from congestive heart failure, complicated by pneumonia. One of her last loving acts toward me was to send for Mister just days before her death, to tell him that no longer could he shirk his responsibilities. She told him that she was dying, that she'd gone as far as she could in preparing me for life, he would now have to pick up where she was leaving off.

Immediately following Mother's funeral, Mister stood on my Papa's back porch and informed me that he would try to find me someplace to go. No longer interested in what he thought of me and wasting no personal insight as to what I thought of him, I quite colorfully, told him what he could do with his offer. The raised hand with which he threatened to punish my impudence was met with a glaring dare from me. Only he could have described accurately what he had seen in my eyes. Whether he had seen blatant hatred or a promise of redress, it caused him to lower his hand.

For the remaining weeks of that school year and into the first few weeks of the new Fall session, Mister did attempt to perform some Father-like duties, which somewhat to his credit, he performed publicly. He signed forms that prevented me from participating in two of my favorite school endeavors, track, and girls' basketball. To be denied those passions by someone of whom I was to claim no relation was bitter. He instead paid for the more lady-like pursuit of piano lessons, which kept me hidden behind walls instead of being on display on a track field or basketball court.

Several more horrendously evil attacks, both physical and emotional, perpetrated against me by two other adult relations precipitated me having to leave my beloved East Texas farm and being placed aboard a train traveling west to California, alone and unsure at 13.

Beyond that day on Papa's back porch, I never had physical contact with Mister again. However, after reaching adulthood, marrying, and obtaining some insightful knowledge as to the sanctity of committed relationships, I reached out to Mister via telephone one early June morning, with the idea of a reconciliation but not expecting one. I, nevertheless, called him. We talked and cried for the larger portion of three hours. He apologized profusely between his own sobs and promised never to put anyone before me again, hoping it wasn't a gesture made too late. I heard the voice of a man broken. A man who admitted to me that he had lived every day since I had left, in agonizing awareness of the grief he had wroth in my young life. He told me that he had kept up with the goings-on of my life through my Mother's brother. He knew before I told him that I was married and asked if I would send a picture of me and my groom. He had heard that I had grown to favor my mother in appearance and to that he offered congratulations. I accepted because I thought my Mother to be beautiful and so obviously, did he.

Although I had placed the call to him, I could not offer him absolution. Instead, I proffered the prospect of a relationship built upon a budding friendship expecting nothing more from each other. As an impetus to the formation of that friendship, I offered, and he accepted my gift of an early Father's Day present in the form of a plane ticket to California. He asked me to allow him a couple of weeks in which to arrange personal matters. I vowed to make the preliminary arrangements and promised to call him again within a week or two with the travel particulars.

I never made that call, yet I did not break my promise. I instead received a call that made mine to him quite unnecessary. My Uncle, my Mother's brother, called with news which proved to me that even as an adult, horrible, hideous things still lurked in the bright light of day. "Hey Aunt Sally," he said. My hand holding the phone began to tremble. No one had called me by that name since before my Mother's death. Still, the passing years had not eased the grip of dread hearing it held for me. I interrupted his attempt at good-natured humor as he tried but failed to ease into whatever it was he had called to tell me. "Unc, just tell me," I pleaded. With a resignation of an audible exhale, my Uncle informed me on that early morning of June 14th of my Father's death some 18 hours earlier by suicide. Long unused, long un-needed, my childhood dark place came rushing forth to rescue me.

Except for hearing the unconfirmed yet unforgettable words detailing the manner of his death, (a shotgun trigger having been tied to his toes with the barrel placed underneath his chin), nothing else registered. Somehow, I'd managed to slog through the remaining hours of that wasted day. I have only one other memory of that day and it was of me standing in my living room, having no recollection of retrieving that day's mail yet there was an envelope in my hands; a return to sender label was attached. The same envelope had earlier been addressed in my handwriting and sent to my father; it contained the picture I had sent to him almost two weeks before. He had never retrieved it from the General Delivery Post Office box.

Days passed without anything to mark their passing. Not too many of them had passed before my husband and I, enroute to the funeral, were shortening the miles separating California from Texas. Upon arrival, I was met by several messengers from the Monster that still occupied Mister's house. Their intent was not to extend condolences but to inform me that I was not welcomed to attend my father's funeral. Further, if I attempted to do so, I would be barred from entering the church that both my Maternal and Paternal grandmothers had helped to establish. I, none too graciously, sent each one of her six hounds back with a message of my own. Tell her, that I am no longer a frightened six-year-old in a darkened laundromat and unless she wants her sickening past revealed at my father's funeral, send me no further messages.

By the time I arrived at the Church the next morning, almost every pew had been filled. There was one pew left with enough room for two of our party of three. I allowed my husband and the other person to occupy those two seats. My intentions were to take a folded chair and sit unnoticed in the back of the church. As is often the case, my intentions did not pan out. My entrance into that small, overcrowded, country church created a ripple of murmuring. "Is that her?" " Are you sure?", "Who is she?", Where has she been?" were just a few of the questions which reached my ears. My whole being screamed at me to be good, to not make waves but I ignored every internal warning! Traveling eighteen-hundred miles in twenty-one hours and being told I was unwelcome did not lend itself toward coercing me to be a good girl. Instead of meekly unfolding the chair and sitting quietly in back, I loudly dragged the still folded chair along the wooden floorboards down the center aisle and unfolded it directly in front of my father's opened casket. Still standing I turned, met her older, still hideous, hate-filled eyes, and silently offered a challenge. I purposely moved my hand to my neck, and she flinched. My hatred of her trumped hers of me this time and she broke eye contact, I'd won! And so, I sat. Whispers and rustling had created a low din and an unspoken expectancy rose within those walls, but I shut it all out; my attention now drawn to my Father's remains and as I stared, searching his head and neck for signs of the trauma they obviously suffered. The stench of Chrysanthemums surrounding his bier almost overpowered me. I was grateful when the service finally ended, and I could escape their scent.

As I exited the church and waited for the coffin to follow, a woman well into her senior years, who I recognized though she not me, tapped me boldly on the shoulder. Her Southern drawled dripped overly sweet from her lips, "Baby, you look familiar, but I just can't place you."

"Yes Ma'am," I said falling back upon my Southern roots.

"I saw you move your chair right up front; you knew him, did you? "she continued.

"Yes Ma'am," was all I allowed her. I suppose not used to having her well-known curiosity so deftly thwarted she took the more direct route.

"Who was he to you, Child?"

"Well, Mrs. (I called her name)," and she was taken aback by my recognition of her without having had the benefit of an intro-duction. She had been one of the Party-line Pariahs so many years before. I smiled openly at her confusion, walked a couple of steps away and called back over my shoulder, not so much to her but to anyone close enough to hear; "He was my Father but, *he told me to Call him Mister.*"

My Brother Was My Keeper...

Faith, Chinee, and Me

Honored by his love, humbled by his vastness, anguished at his departure, and grateful for the memories. I dedicate this to Mr. J.B. Allen, (Chinee to those who loved him most) My BROTHER.

There was never a day when I first "met" him. Quite simply, he was just always there, and I expected him always to be so. He was a part of my life before I knew life. He was a part of me, before I was me. He impacted my life. He was my surrogate father, my counselor, my confidante, and my best friend, He was my brother.

One of my earliest most significant memories of my brother took place on my school's playground when I was 6 years old. My best friend at the time was Faith Dixon. I loved this little girl as much as I loved chocolate cake, which took some doing! She inhaled, I exhaled. If she stubbed her toe, I cried. When I was hungry, we both ate. She was a petite little thing, much smaller than the other first graders, with a slight but adorably, endearing speech impediment. Faith was my bosom buddy, my lifelong pal, ma petit amie, and whether she knew it or not, she belonged wholly to me.

This particular memory took place during our first morning recess on a late spring day. Faith and I were doing our usual arm in arm, skipping about the playground dance when I declared, without preamble, "I love chocolate milk," to which Faith replied, "I yuv chocomilk too!" Immediately my affectionate sentiments drifted to colors. "I love yellow," (and still do), and Faith sweetly responded, "I yuv yelyo too!" It was at that exact moment when my vision captured a movement at about fifty yards or better to my right, toward the high school end of the school. (*Wiergate School was a one stop for all school, encompassing grades 1 through 12 with undrawn but definitive lines separating the 1st and 2nd grade classrooms from the 3rd through 7th and these from the 8th through 12th classrooms. It was a highly functioning class system; yes, pun intended*). I saw the handsome, adorable, smiling face of my brother walking across campus toward the science building. In the same sing-song manner in which I had voiced my two pre-vious affections, I began, "There goes my brother and I love him more than anything," and just as she had mimicked the two pre-vious statements, no doubt having gained my silent permission to do so, Faith began to repeat, "There goes my brudda, and I..."

What followed was the most one-sided, knockdown, drag out fight which was as out of the blue as an Arizona snowstorm in August! My dear darling friend had crossed a line of which even I did not know existed. I do not know how much time had passed or how long Faith lay cowering on the ground terrified in the face of my absolute anger as I stood there stoically resolute in my belief that I had fought off the true enemy of the "Big brother/ little sister relationship"! I stood there ready to again defend that relationship, until I felt myself being lifted ever so swiftly by my right arm, (had it not been for this macabre intervention, would I have dealt the death blow with my angry little fist?). Not only were my feet being lifted off the ground, I began to feel a fierce unfamiliar stinging on the calves of my legs. What in God's cre-ation could this possibly be, A SWITCH??????!!!!!!! This was about as underhanded a sneak attack as could be imagined!

Looking over and back to where my right shoulder should have been, was a face that was malevolently intent on teaching a lesson more complex than my 6 years of experience could ever begin to comprehend. Mrs. Adams, that loathsome harbinger of impending suffering to all who dared to enter the primer grades, had placed a death grip on my wrist with her left hand and was none too politely flogging the living hell out of me with her right. You must understand that my keen mind and sharp wit had yet to develop by this age and being so lacking, I was refused even a glimmer of suspicion as to why this woman was attacking me, nor was I left with any clues as to how to quickly bring about a cessation of this action! (Had Faith had the same thoughts just moments earlier?). With a simple thought of self-preservation, I did what would come naturally to any self-respecting 6-year-old; I screamed and screamed loudly and repeatedly! This befuddled the old crone long enough to cause her to loosen her grip and momentarily halt my flagellation with that formidable switch, (where in heaven's name had she found a switch on a playground devoid of trees anyway?) She generally carried a gigantic pencil of which was often applied forcefully against the head of a wayward first grader. In this case, that pencil would have been infinitely more preferable, had I been given that benevolent choice.

In my wildest imaginings, in the whole of my whimsical thoughts, or even in the midst of my most embellished dreams could I have spoken what happened next! I daresay, at that precise moment my only thought was, "it's about damn time!"

Faith stood up on those tiny little legs and ran as if her dress was on fire; calling out to MY BROTHER, yelling for him to help ME. There was only one other person who was more incredulous than me at this change of circumstances, Mrs. Brown! Soon, it was as if Gabriel and his host had descended upon that playground when my BROTHER arrived with half the football team following him and bringing up the rear, on tired but determined little legs, was Faith! At this point, I began to feel a bit sorry for old lady Brown, but she needed to be taught a lesson in elementary protocol. Not bothering to say a word, my brother simply yet purposely plucked me from Mrs. Brown's hand, sat down on the hard-packed, sun baked red clay of that little Texas playground and cradled me. Nothing more profound than that but it was the world being laid at my feet. He was my Polydeuces and I, his Helen. Mrs. Brown, that bastion of first graders' nightmares, shrank in the presence of my brother's unshakable rage for her and his unwavering love for me.

Then there stood Faith, gently rubbing away the angry welts Mrs. Brown's switch had left upon my legs saying, "Hur wasn't hurting me, Miz. Brown, hur was just paying with me". WOW!

It was all too soon summer vacation, and it would be almost five decades before I would meet Faith again, her family had suddenly and without notice, moved away. I missed her but more importantly, I forgave her for taking so long to get help, but not for claiming my brother as her own! (Yes, it would seem I was once an awful self- righteous little waif).

But these musings are not about Faith and me, as odd as that may seem. They are however, about one of the first loves of my life. Thank you for allowing me to present to you with venerated pleasure and unabashed pride the subject of many of my ruminations, the occupier of many of my memories, the embellisher of my life. Please enjoy meeting...My BROTHER, Chinee, aka J.B Allen.

MY BROTHER WAS MY KEEPER...

The Trees, Chinee, and Me

The early 1960's were a little more sophisticated than the 50's; a little less naive, a bit more idealistic, but still full of morality, conventionality, and hardworking ethics. It was a time of hope and determinate objectivity, when almost everyone felt a sense of possibility.

Nowhere was this felt more keenly than in the hallowed halls of Wiergate High School. That citadel of education, a stronghold of mores. The place where seeds of hope were planted. The defenders of that hope were the selfless members of staff at this, The Home of the Panthers, dutifully led by Principal, Artie Brailsford, and Coach and Ag teacher David Snell, who was also an occasional Bus Driver, if needed. These two virtuous men aimed primarily to keep the flame of hope lit. And "lit" you would be were you ever caught outside the bounds of what they deemed fitting for young people under their tutelage.

It was during these times when someone, somewhere decided that our idle hands and minds would culminate in Satan serving us up as dessert on his lunch tray. Therefore, it was decreed that young men be kept engaged, not only during the hours in the custodial care of the school's staff but afterwards as well and it appeared that the "someone" had the full blessing of not only Messieurs Brailsford and Snell but the parents as well.

Although we attended school in the township of Wiergate, we actually lived within the community of Shankleville, a settlement of roughly 4000 acres of Piney woods, creeks, farmland, two cemeteries, three churches, about thirty-five families, and absolutely nothing else. Everyone knew everyone and if the person standing next to you was not related to you then the person standing next to him was a cousin to you both.

There was little to give flight to a young man's fancy there in Shankleville. Many an evening was spent by these young men mimicking the nocturnal call of the forlorn sounding Whippoorwill. Lazy afternoons might find some of them challenging each other to a fast swim across a pond guarded enthusiastically by water moccasins and rattlers or less exciting to be sure, filching pears and plums from neighboring farms. So, it was armed with this knowledge of the possible summertime redundancy for these young men, when the guardians of unguarded minds, bent to keep idleness at bay by forcing young men or perhaps better, forcibly encouraging Mr. Snell to instruct every young man under his guidance, to plant five thousand pine trees each. That was five thousand trees EACH. I did not understand it as a curious but silent six-year-old nor do I now all these many years later why would anyone with even a modicum of foresight, insist on planting more than fifty thousand trees in a small area within the Piney Woods of East Texas, where one would find it extremely difficult if not impossible, to fall forward and not scrape pine bark off the nearest tree as one fell? As a matter of fact, it was more likely that you would fall and never hit the ground, so thick were the trees. But planting it would be or lose a semester grade. Some of the young men thoughts leaned more toward accepting the loss of a grade rather than toil in the vapid, dense humidity of a Gulf Coast summer. Chinee chose to plant and after what seemed like hours and hours of pleading to be allowed to help, he finally acquiesced. Isn't it funny how older siblings are so adept at getting you to plead with them to allow you to do something of which they wanted you to do all along and then be gracious enough as to allow you to thank them for going through the trouble? I waited years to try this handy logic on unsuspecting nieces and nephews, but I was never as good at using it as Chinee had been.

And so, the planting began, hour after hour, day after day and week after week. On our knees and all fours, using our index and middle fingers to bore into the soft red earth, we gently planted one sapling at a time and replaced the soil by mounding it ever so slightly for support. It took four full weeks from start to finish. Mother only have kiddingly, threatened to bill the school for the knee patches she would need to mend the holes in our britches. Five thousand trees in four weeks, but what a wonderful month it had been, just the Trees, Chinee, and me! He told me so much about his outlook on life and he taught me things of which I would have never learned otherwise; things like what a line of scrimmage was. (Of course, we talked football, it was East Texas after all). I learned the meaning of 1ST and 10, off-sides, quarterback sneak, pass interference, blitz, screen pass, safeties, formation, a kick return, man in motion, fumble, illegal formation, offense, and defense. He drilled me on positions like quarterback, pass defender, tight-end, wide receiver, special team, fullback, halfback, defensive back, corner back and hurry back! Chinee taught me every possible pass play and running play in that little book he carried everywhere, along with defensive and offensive moves. I learned every player and position on the field. There was just one thing that I did not learn while we served as the Prince and Princess of our tiny Kingdom of Pines and that was...

...*__HOW TO PLAY FOOTBALL!__*

MY BROTHER WAS MY KEEPER...

The Tackle, Chinee, and Me

Being the only boy in a family of women held special meaning for Chinee. He was born smack in the middle of four girls. Two older protective, adoring sisters and two hero worshiping younger ones and a mother who took adoration of an only son to a different level entirely. Theirs' was a special relationship. There was nothing collectively, that we thought was too good for him. Chinee seldom asked for anything for himself but there was always plenty giving going on; either by the five of us to him or him to the five of us. He took his title of family patriarch earnestly and emotively. There was only one thing wrong with this picture as far as he could see, there was no one to help him practice his football plays. (Personally, all and all, I thought he had it pretty damn good but that was just a little kid's perspective).

Chinee's intentions were to try out for the school's football team in the Fall and was actually pretty much a shoe-in. He already had shoulders so wide that even at 13, shoulder pads were mere accessories. His full height of 6 feet had already been reached and he had obtained a girth that demanded attention. Coach Snell had anticipatorily given him a copy of a playbook, but he needed someone to help him run the plays. He wanted to be certain he knew every play in that book before school started but he could not very well set up a Wing-T offensive play alone or pass and receive to himself (keep this in mind, it become very important later). Seeing my brother's predicament, I once again thought to come to his rescue and tried to devise ways in which to help him. Suddenly or maybe not so suddenly, Chinee was *agreeing* that I could help although I was not cognizant of ever asking him if I could, (Boy oh Boy, he was good).

The first order of business was learning how to throw a ball. You really have to try and picture this in order to appreciate the momentous assignment of which I had been given or asked for, depending on whom you choose to believe. I was perhaps forty-five pounds of knobby knees, spindly legs, ungainly arms, and terribly small hands. For any other assignment, my hands would have been called delicate, but for football tossing however, they were simply called terribly small. I remember Chinee telling me something about putting my index finger on the seam and my thumb somewhere making an L-shape or some such thing...It really did not matter because none of what he directed me to do was physically possible for me anyway. Just seeing the disappointment in Chinee's face was enough for me to give it the old school try. I grabbed the ball with both hands as one would an axe handle and after a few hundred tries, I executed a pinpoint bomb accurate to fifteen yards. THE GAME WAS ON! I passed to the left. I passed to the right. There were a couple of lateral passes and a flea flicker or two. The grin on my brother's face at the end of those exercises could have bought gold.

In his excitement to run more plays, I think he must have forgotten to give me a lesson or two. My next feat was to learn how to catch passes. Chinee grabbed the ball and ran backwards about 15 yards and threw a bullet. It was a thing of beauty the way he sent that ball literally spiraling toward me. I stood there mesmerized watching that perfectly thrown, brown bomb; that is until the end of the ball nailed me right on the sternum and down, I went, hard!

I was to learn later that his pinpoint, accurate drilling of that ball into my chest was called "placing the ball on the numbers," but I felt more like my number was up. To put it quite simply, it hurt.

He ran to me and helped me up, apologized profusely and offered to quit practice when it appeared obvious to him that I was having trouble breathing. I just could not be the reason my brother did not make the team, so I did my best Bucky Buck Up routine and carried on in grand style. This time he showed me how to catch the ball by cradling it with my arms. (This was a lesson which should have been taught one bruised sternum ago). Five or ten tries at this and I was diving and jumping for passes, no one could say that I was not a quick and determined student.

It was on the next pass when the continued longevity of my life became seriously doubtful. Chinee threw a thirty-yard pass, which I caught and suddenly he morphed from offensive to defensive without bothering to tell me the difference. There were no shouts of Run Girl Run! There was no bleating to fall and protect my position, (we had not covered this part yet so I wouldn't have known what the hell the yelling would have been about anyway). I do know that I saw all one hundred and eighty-five pounds of my brother coming at me faster than I'd ever seen anyone move before. My honest thought was that he wanted the ball from me quickly so that we could get one last play in before darkness fell, and darkness was my next true non-technicolor vision. TACKLED is what he called it, (a word of which until then had not made it into any of my previous lessons). ATTEMPTED MURDER is what it really was!

Ok, now I understood. I shook it off, (after about 10 minutes or so). I re-inflated my lungs, wiped the snot and tears from my face and tried it again. Man, what a lesson he taught me that evening. He tossed me a little flea flicker from about the twenty and started a full-on rush. When that ball touched my hands that time, I turned on my heels and ran toward my goal, away from his goal, away from a second sure-fire tackle, away from him and everything football with such swiftness that Wilma Rudolph running the 200 meter in Rome would have been hard pressed to catch me. As an adult, I would look back on that day and that lesson and remember all the times life had tackled me without warning. That day, that lesson bolstered me as an adult, to know that I needed no longer to run from those who would tackle or blindside me. As an adult, with few exceptions, I have stood and defended my goal. Being tackled or blindsided by something thrown my way is no longer blindly accepted.

As I ran away from Chinee and that tackle, somewhere from yards behind me, I heard what had for all time sounded like music to me. I had always loved the sound of Chinee's full throated, rising up from the depths of his belly, stopping in his chest just long enough to get an extra breath to allow it burst forward loudly, laughter. The sound of it followed me until I felt safe and finally stopped running. It was music to me and as I think back, thankfully...

♬ I can still hear him laughing. ♬

My Brother Was My Keeper...

The Dime, Chinee, and Me

Since I was the youngest, there was always someone escorting me everywhere. Except on our acreage, I was never allowed to venture anywhere on my own. This included Sunday school, regular school, or visiting our neighbors, understandably since the nearest neighbor was almost two miles away. My sister closest to me in age was five years older and my Brother was older by seven, so I was most often joined to one of their hips, much to the consternation of my sister. It was a feather in my cap to have had two older siblings in school with me. It kept being bullied to a minimum and I was not opposed to playing the, *"I'm going to tell my sister or my brother card"*. No sir, I did not mind that card at all; I felt any owned asset should be used and used wisely. Older siblings were also good for filching a cookie or two every once in a while; especially when Mother did not quite agree that a cookie would settle my too often upset stomach. Those times, Chinee would walk past my sick bed ever so slyly and deposit a cookie as quick as you please into my anxious hands and away from Mother's unsuspecting eyes. Since I was sick anyway why be denied a bit of pleasure? You must already know how much better many things are when you're sneaking them and to have my hero, my big brother, being the one to deliver this small object of my desire was like having chocolate with my chocolate. Was there ever a better brother?

Occasionally, there were times when Mother would pull one of my siblings out of school for extra help around the farm. If it was for help needed inside the home, my sister would be asked to stay. If the chore required more strength and out-of-doors stamina, Chinee would stay. It was the quirky mischievous humor of Fate which determined that on this particular school day, my sister would be too ill to attend school and Mother needed Chinee's help.

I must explain something here and now so as not to confuse you in later chapters. My two eldest sisters were 13 and 16 years older than me and were out of the family home and on their own before I started school. So pretty much throughout my entrance into my teens, it was just the three of us youngest kids growing up together.

This particular joke of Fate left me alone to climb aboard that which was never before but now became a frighteningly alarming, humongous, flesh eating, body snatching, bully concealing school bus! I actually felt lightheaded at the prospect of leaving the warmth and loving inter-sanctum of my house and being driven away in that yellow rattletrap. What kind of silly errand would cause a Mother to abandon her youngest child to the cruel, lonely world of singularity? I wasn't even sure if I could find the way to my classroom alone. And who would walk me to the bus that afternoon? Did not anyone know that there were millions of buses in that yard after school and, blast it, they ALL LOOKED THE SAME? (*there were actually only two or 3 buses most days, but still*). How would I know which one to board? Was Mother really tired of me, was she hoping I would board the wrong bus and be dropped off in parts unknown? I wasn't much trouble at home, I really did not eat much, and my sister was the one who awakened me most mornings to comb &

dress my hair before school thereby freeing Mother to do other things. I could not think of one reason why Mother would do this to me! I had not cried or been an obvious bother for at least a couple of weeks; my shoes were dusted each night and I put my clothes away without being told. I gathered the eggs every day before and after school, didn't I? (And what a terrifying event that was! I am terrified of a living and walking chicken to this very day! I am absolutely certain that the only cure for a fearless, clucking, chasing chicken is a bag of well-seasoned flour and a vat of hot oil).

I washed the dishes twice a week and raked the yard every time it needed it. Mother needed me, I know she needed me yet, she was setting me up for a future episode, (30 years later), of "What ever happened to..." Who would lick the cake batter bowl and beaters if I wasn't there? Maybe that wasn't a good example, my sister would still be there of course. Then who would help Mother wrap the presents at Christmas? That wasn't a winnable argument either because yup, my sister again. MOTHER DID NOT NEED ME! SHE REALLY DID NOT NEED ME! The switch was flipped, and I saw the light. I was walking the plank, sent out to pasture, deserted, casted off, dumped! I was dispensable and the big, yellow bus would attend to the dispensing. My whole body began to shake and shutter. The thought of never again having a cookie was an even worse thought than being face to face with the bullies on the bus...alone! Be that as it may, I determined to face my fate as the trooper I was meant to be, if I could only get rid of the urge to wet my britches! (All of my life in time of stress and life altering moments, my bladder has always failed me. It had begun a day long ago in a dimly lit laundromat.) Even on the day of my wedding-after I had been trussed up, tied, and sucked in, being escorted down the aisle, I had to make a quick dash to the nearest Ladies room. On the way to the hospital to give birth to my first son, contractions five minutes apart,

I needed to stop at a nearby gas station. At my youngest son's wedding as they were about to announce my entry, I was doing a "Lou-Lou Skip to My Lou" jiggle adjustment all the way back from the ladies' room toward the church's center aisle, barely making it back in time.

As I was contemplating whether going to the outhouse would be the solution to my immediate problem, I felt a hand on my shoulder. I looked up expecting to see a hatchet aimed at my skull, (at least that would be a kinder method of getting rid of me, I thought) but instead, I saw the understanding face of my brother. How long had he been watching me? Had the rattling of my bones alerted him to my distress, or had he just intuitively known all along how this would affect me? He leaned down and kissed the top of my head; my knees buckled, and my heart melted; He then reached inside his pocket and brought out the dullest, most beat up, saddest looking mercury dime there could possibly be in circulation and he gave it to me. He made me promise to buy two packages of cookies from the School's 5-cent cookie machine. One, I was to buy when I first got to school to have with my lunch (if I survived the trip there) and the second at the end of the school day on my way back to the bus, (if I found the right darn bus), that one I was to share with him when I got home. Thusly, he taught me that a little bit of sugar will sweeten any bitter cup.

Still now, the best way I know to show my love when my friends or family members have troubles, is by whipping up a cake, a pie, or a batch of cookies to comfort them.

Surprisingly, no one tortured me unnecessarily that first day I was alone at school. Well, Ronnie did do his best to annoy me, but a handful of playground dirt thrown into his eyes stopped that. Miss Thelma, our bus driver, did not suddenly morph into whatever a pre-1980's Freddie Kruger would be. I even found my way to the correct bus that afternoon. Malachi did not pull my hair from the seat behind me on the bus and we got home without anything horrible happening.

Chinee was waiting for me at the swing that hung from one of the two grand, stately Sycamore trees framing our house. I ran to him so happy to be shed of my "be a big Girl" edit and I was rewarded by being picked up, swung around, hugged, and placed upon the two by four board seat of my rope swing. He knelt beside the swing, asked me about my day and as I recounted it proudly, I shared the Tom's peanut butter sandwich cookies paid for with his sad pitiful dime. Oh, what a bright, special memory that dull, little dime bought for us as we sat under that tree.

Oh yes by the way, my Mother still needed me after all, she made me rake the yard and gather the evening eggs that day. And for all my trouble, she even served Fried Chicken for dinner! What a day! What a delicious day.

My Brother Was My Keeper...

The Spring, Chinee, and Me

Life for us took place on 57 acres of useable farmland; an average size for the area and time in which we lived, many had far more acreage, many had far less. Even so, we only used about 20 acres to produce and provide crops for both our family and the livestock. At various times that livestock included: horses, pigs, chickens, turkeys, and every once and a while a cow or two.

Everything we did was by design and clockwork. This was made even more difficult because we had no access to running water. We relied totally on the graciousness of God and nature to irrigate the fields, orchards, garden, and to provide water for the animals. But we had to rely on simple backbreaking, manual labor to provide water for our intimate and personal needs: drinking, laundry, and bath water. It did not seem so terribly laborious at the time because it was all that we knew, however now, having been exposed and accustomed to indoor plumbing lo these many years, it's difficult to imagine how we actually managed to get along without it.

Every Tuesday was "washday." Our day began at dawn hauling water from the creek to fill our wringer washer, which sat looming and unquenchable on our back porch. We also had to fill the two #3 galvanize tubs needed to rinse the laundry after it had been beaten into submission by an unyielding agitator. At the end of the wash cycle, we would guide the washed but sat-urated laundry, piece by piece, into a medieval torture device called a roller to squeeze away soapy wash water and prepare for their rinsing. The #3 tubs were the types used for the much more enjoyable past time of bobbing for apples. Between the washer, the galvanized tubs, and the huge, black, iron pot we used to boil and disinfect our white linens and personal items, it could take upwards of 70 gallons of water to complete this weekly task. No modern appliance has ever produced a whiter, fresher, or more sanitized batch of laundry than that old smoke pot which is really quite ironic and amusing giving how dirty & soot encrusted that old pot was. Never judge anything by its outward appearance.

Huge barrels were placed strategically around the farm to catch and hold rainwater. This water was used mainly for per-sonal cleaning and for our livestock. But every morning & after-noon, before and after school, rain, or shine, in blistering heat or icy cold, we had to walk the half mile, the last 1/8 of it, down a steep decline to a natural bubbling, self-filtering, cold water spring. It was the job of us three kids to make sure that our Mother and Grandparents had enough water for drinking, coffee making, and cooking throughout the day. My Papa's serious coffee addiction notwithstanding, we could usually get by on just one trip each to the spring per the twice daily sessions. We accomplished this by Chinee carrying two 2-gallon buckets, my sister carrying one 1-gallon bucket and I was proudly, the deliv-erer of my grandfather's coffeepot water, which I did by car-rying a small, recycled Steen's syrup can. It held a bit more than a quart and the can itself was about six inches tall and had per-haps a four-inch opening. Laugh if you like, but that little bucket became impossibly weighty and the bail cut deeply into my small fingers as I endeavored to climb that steep hill without losing its contents. To spill its contents, meant going back down that treacherous hill, filling the container again and quite possibly trudging back up alone. If you could not keep up, you could be left behind.

On one winter morning at precisely 4:30 a.m. as was normal, Monday through Friday without fail, the temperature outside had fallen below freezing and the temperature inside the farmhouse seemed even colder! Mother had already given us the first warning call to up and at 'em as Papa was just beginning to get our old wood-burning heater fired up. Even the smell of something warm and sweet drifting in from the kitchen was not enough to persuade us to crawl from beneath the piles of woolen blankets and heavy handmade quilts which were so far, supplying the only warmth in the house.

We groaned at the booming sound of our grandfather's voice announcing the second and final warning to "GET UP." We hit the floor and raced toward the heater, holding blankets around us. After warming somewhat, we dressed in as many layers as possible to protect ourselves against frigid weather and still allowed for movement. By the time we were finished washing up, brushing our teeth, dressing, and putting a heavy protective layer of Vaseline on our faces, the sun would be yawning, stretching, and trying to figure out why the heck he or anybody else was bothering to get up this early on such a cold, cold morning

Four pairs of socks and 2 pair of pants for Chinee along with several tee shirts, a mackinaw, a heavy wool coat, a bib cap with ear flaps and he was ready for the trek to the spring. I really did not care what my sister wore because whatever she had on would not warm me one whit; but I would be allowed to walk with at least one of my hands in Chinee's warm coat pockets. Pants for little girls were not yet popular and as such they were not easily obtained. Therefore, I was dressed in at least 2 old woolen shifts, the better to keep out the wind, 2 pairs of tights, at least 3 pairs of socks on my feet and another 3 on my hands (no mittens did we have). I tied an extra-long scarf around my head and neck and finished with a sweater and coat. The only real difference between myself and a mummy, other than the obvious, would have been that a mummy would have moved infinitely more graceful inside its swaddling.

The trip down the hill was beyond treacherous because it had no steps carved into it. There were no railings or ropes onto which to hold and assist our progress. There were only uneven footholds created by years of use and overgrown limbs and branches on which to hold. The ground was slippery with sheets of ice and the falling sleet pricked our faces. Undaunted and focused on the task at hand, we dared not tarry.

Arriving at the spring first, Chinee dropped his bucket onto the frozen surface to break the thick layer of ice which had formed overnight. The sound of metal meeting ice reverberated and echoed throughout the still, silent morning. He carefully filled my sister's bucket first and passed it back to her. He repeated the task for me. Lastly, he filled his two muscle fatiguing pails and we headed for home. If we had thought the trip downhill was treacherous; the trip uphill was damn near life threatening. It was almost next to impossible to gain any purchase on the icy slope and one misstep could cause us to go sliding backwards downhill. As Chinee led the way breaking a path into the ice for us to follow, my sister would match his footsteps and I would follow in hers. I was mere steps from the top as I began to slide uncontrollably. I could not regain my balance regardless of how many branches I reached out to for stability. I fell hard on the frozen ground and slid backwards the total way down the hill, spilling my bucket of water over my clothes as I went. Bruised, scared, and half frozen at the bottom of the hill, I laid crying from pain and embarrassment. The water had spilled on my dress and caused it to freeze and splay out from my body almost instantly. I had on so many layers of clothing that I could not right myself on my own. My sister stood at the top of the hill yelling grumpily for me to get up because she was cold and wanted to get home, (as if I wasn't and wanted something different than she—older sisters, geez). Chinee yelled at her to go home and that we'd follow. He sat his huge buckets down on the top of the hill, the water in them quickly turning to ice, and headed downhill for me. He made it to me safely. He righted me first then retrieved my bucket to refill it. He then picked me up and placed me piggyback on his body and climbed again the hill. He did not put me on the ground when he reached the top. He simply asked me if I could now hold my little bucket, to which I answered yes. Not only did he carry his two buckets of water but me and my bucket on his back as well and he never once complained.

So, what is the lesson here, you're probably wondering? Well, it was that no matter how far I ever fell, no matter how slippery the slope, no matter what troubles I found myself surrounded by, no matter how cold or dark the situation, Chinee was always there to help pick me up and carry the load.

Without a doubt, without a single lifelong doubt, I loved my brother but even more undoubtedly, I KNOW that he loved me.

MY BROTHER WAS MY KEEPER...

The Hospital, Chinee, and Me

Although I stated in an earlier chapter that these writings were not completely about me, I must quantify that statement now by saying that this chapter will be almost totally about me. I apologize for this because I do not find myself nearly as interesting as my brother and I am quite uncomfortable being anywhere other than in background situations. However, to cycle back to having him as the center of attention, I must digress momentarily, but only for the rendering of the next two chapters.

May 3rd, 1967; I was twelve and excitedly anticipating the passing of the next three weeks and thereby falling headlong into summer vacation. Adding to my excitement was the very recent arrival of my two eldest sisters, visiting from Los Angeles. The house was full of activity and preparation. The only thing that marred this happy time was the fact that our mother had been only recently released from a lengthy hospitalization due to a serious bout of pneumonia; this in conjunction with a heart weakened by congested heart failure kept everyone on alert. We were all taking extra precautions to keep her as quiet and stress free as possible. It was a rare occasion for the five of us siblings to be under the same roof at the same time. The last time had been for the funeral of my grandmother 3 years previously. I don't ever recall a time before then.

My mother was a beautiful woman. She stood approximately 5'7", had a smooth, unblemished, rich, caramel complexion, large and haunting eyes that angled down almost imperceptibly on the inside corners. A shock of silver hair slightly off center helped to highlight her oval shaped face. Utterly unaware of her beauty, she was only 44 years old and looked forward to her birthday exactly three weeks away. We were, or at least everyone else was, busy planning a 45th birthday celebration for her. Since I was the youngest, I was more of a nuisance than a help to anyone so, I was not included in the majority of the planning unless it entailed running and fetching.

We confidently expected that since her birthday was still three weeks away, Mother would have ample time to recover and would be able to enjoy the first birthday party of her life. We were all looking forward to it and Mother insisted she would be well in time to help in the preparation of the party food.

We had all been up for hours, laughing and enjoying being in each other presence when someone noticed, probably Mother, that it was getting close to the time for the arrival of the school bus. I was sitting next to mother telling her of my plans for the day, when suddenly a violent coughing spell overwhelmed her. Struggling to control her breathing left her so weakened and her appearance so diminished that something akin to terror crept into my soul, filled me with panic, and joltingly brought back to mind a dream I'd had a month earlier, just prior to mother getting ill.

In my dream, I was unbearably upset because my three sisters were all wearing beautiful white dresses and I was dressed in an olive and cream three-piece suit. I felt totally separated and excluded from whatever occasion we were dressing. Mother was even wearing white. Chinee was dressed in a crisp black suit and wearing the whitest, brightest dress shirt ever made. (Obviously, that old smoke pot was doing its' job even in my dream). We were

56

all in church; everyone was so pretty, but sad and I could not figure it out until my dream did that "poof" thing that dreams do and we were all suddenly someplace else. I was standing now in the cemetery nearest our home and everyone was not only looking sad but weeping openly. I looked around for my siblings because I had somehow become separated from them. I could not see over the heads of the people in front of me, so I looked down instead and saw an open grave, but oddly there was water filling the grave ever so slowly. As I looked about to see if anyone other than me was witnessing this phenomenon, there appeared a coffin directly in front of me; it was being opened eerily and slowly as the crowd began to sing Pass Me Not O Gentle Savior. Reluctantly, I looked into the coffin only to see Mother's smiling face with her beautiful haunting eyes closed tightly, almost as if sealed.

I had awakened to my own screams and ran to my Mother's bedroom sobbing uncontrollably as I recounted the details of my dream. She pulled me into her arms and comforted me by reading a scripture from the Bible she kept at her bedside table. St. John 14th chapter, *"Let not your heart be troubled, ye believe in God, believe also in me. In my Father's house are many mansions. If it were not so, I would have told you. I go to prepare a place for you and if I go to prepare a place for you, I will come again and receive you unto myself, so that where I am there you may be also"*. She made me promise that whenever I felt sad or lost when thinking of her, I would remember this passage, I promised and fell list-lessly asleep in her arms as she hummed, *Pass me Not, O Gentle Savior, hear my humble cry, whilst on others thou are calling, do not pass me by.*

I did not want to get on that bus that Wednesday morning. I did not know why, but I felt that my mother's very life depended on me remaining there at home with her. I pleaded with her to let me stay but she just squeezed my hand and told me that she would see me later and to make sure that I accomplished all the plans that I had made for the day. I got on the bus that morning filled with an un-named dread but determined to do as my mother asked.

Sometime within the 2nd period, I was summoned to the principal's office; when I walked into Professor Brailsford's office I was met by the Girl's Principal and my eldest sister. That awful dread from earlier had returned and I demanded to know where Mother was. My sister told me that mother was in the car waiting. It seems, she said, Mother had a doctor's appointment that day and did not know how long it would take. She did not want me to come home from school and not find her there. What no one told me was that Mother's condition had gotten progressively worse in the few hours since I'd boarded the bus that morning and she was being taken to the hospital's Emergency Room. My guess was that Mother remembered my distress from earlier and was still worried about my state of mind and thought to make the stop at school to alleviate any fear I might have. My sister was there to tell me that if they had not returned home by the time school was over, I was not to worry. She told me that my youngest sister would be at home waiting. Further, she explained, accompanying her on the drive to the doctor, would be my second eldest sister and Chinee. I did not trust something about the tone of her voice. She had never used so many words to explain anything to anyone, EVER. I refused to return to class and was extremely close to having a public meltdown and my old friend Headache had come to visit and brought her friend Darkness with her. Had Professor Brailsford and his ever-present razor strap been standing before me at that moment, neither would have deterred my insistence on accompanying my siblings and Mother.

We lived in the very easternmost portion of East Texas. We were only about 10 miles from the Louisiana border where the

Sabine River separated the two states. My Mother's physician was on staff at a hospital in Merryville, Louisiana, approximately 45 minutes away and this was our immediate destination. One other thought to note: this was the South in 1967, where the Civil Rights war was still being fiercely fought by those on both sides who refused to surrender. This day was to find us, my siblings, my Mother, and me all in a losing battle of that war.

By the time we arrived at the hospital, the fluid in Mother's lungs was making it difficult for her to breathe. The heavy air, the dreary sky that promised rain, and the oppressive humidity added to the wretchedness of our mission. As we entered the emergency room, there were no other patients waiting to be seen, still we were told to be seated. We waited about fifteen minutes as Mother's breathing became audibly labored. One of my sisters, I do not remember which, approached the nurse's station again, mere footsteps from us and pleaded for help, but at that very moment a Caucasian gentleman was brought in by a co-worker, to have a sliver of metal removed from his left palm.

They laughed and one joked about what a stroke of good luck it had been for the injured man to have gotten the sliver in his left hand because since he was left-handed, he had needed to be driven to the hospital. If they timed things exactly right, he said, they could actually stretch this into an all-afternoon, excused absence from work. They laughed and flirted with the nurse to whom my sister was speaking and by whom she was now ignored. As another nurse passed us, my sister asked her if she would please help mother. She scolded us in a condescending tone saying that there were real people that really needed help and we should mind our manners and not disturb the other patients. We watched helplessly as "The Sliver Man" was called in and had his wound attended. As the joviality continued among the two co-workers and the two nurses, mother, without warning, collapsed and fell to the floor. There were screams reverberating throughout the hospital corridor. I don't know if my voice joined those of my other siblings, but my throat was raw and hoarse later. There were sounds of running footsteps and I heard someone say, "There's a bunch of Niggras keeping up a ruckus and ought to be taught a lesson on how to act around proper folks! How dare they disturb good decent folks and all?"

It was only then that my mother was finally attended to, sort of. She was placed in a room and promptly ignored again. The three of us girls helped mother undress as Chinee waited in the corridor. I silently worried about him and prayed because he was out there alone with those people who were angry about our pleadings for help. As mother lay on the bed with eldest sister on her right and second eldest on the left, I stood at the foot of the bed as we all worked in wordless harmony to speed the undressing process. They lifted her upper body from behind to remove her blouse as I leaned toward her from the foot of the bed and held her hands helping her to sit upright. Barely able to keep my toes on the floor my thin arms strained in their mission. I was looking at my sisters as they removed Mother's blouse when my hands began to ache horribly. It felt as if my bones were being crushed. I looked at my hands as if they were not a part of me and tried to figure out from where the pain was coming. I looked at Mother's hands surrounding mine and I could see the veins in her hand raised and blue, I wanted to scream out in pain but quickly remembered the warning of the people in the lobby. I looked up into Mother's face and unbidden terror gripped my soul! Mother's face was unrecognizable. Her beautiful features were both flattened and swollen simultaneously. Her lovely, slightly slanted eyes were unseeing and bulging unnaturally from their sockets. I'd never seen it, but intuitively knew exactly what the face of a person being hanged must look like. I imagined it to also be akin to the look of a person drowning, which is what my mother was doing. It was not the peaceful letting go as portrayed on television or in the movies; it was horrific. Mother was literally drowning in front me and my hands seemed to be her lifeline. God, if only I could have breathed for her, if I could have but loaned her my own air, but those were thoughts that came later. I cannot remember what my thoughts were at the time, beyond the pain in my hands, the immediate fear and sense of impending, everlasting loss.

I suppose that the stiffening of her body alerted my sisters to her distress because I had become totally mute in my fear. This time, I knew for sure that it was my sisters and not me who broke the silence of that room with screams of desperation. This time, nurses and doctors rushed in with a crash cart and yelled for us to get out the room. I could not leave, not because I was intent on being disobedient but because my hands were locked in my Mother's death grip. I wanted to go yet I felt guilty for wanting to. I did not know how to help mother and felt ashamed of myself that I could not. I hated my sisters for not only leaving Mother but also for appearing to not give me a second thought. From afar off I heard Chinee yelling at them as to my whereabouts, but I still could not speak. I remember the nurses kept pushing mother back down on the bed and with seemingly superhuman strength she kept sitting up trying to breathe, and with each of their pushes her grip on my hands pulled me further onto the bed with her; my feet finally leaving the precarious purchase my toes had made. It was then that one of the attendants, finally noticing me, roughly grabbed me around the waist and practically threw me from the room thus breaking the lifeline between mother and child.

Many recurring nightmares over many years always left me wondering if breaking my grip with Mother hastened her death. I suppose it was my childish and unconscious attempt to accept blame. For years afterwards, fear and uncertainty made it extremely difficult to hold another person's hand.

In the corridor, there was no sound to muffle the hushed, hurried, and doubtful whispers coming from room number 7, Mother's room. There were the squeaks of the wheels on the lunch carts as the lunch trays were being returned to the hospital cafeteria. There was the distant ringing of telephones and the fierce pounding of my own heartbeat in my ears. But the sound that was most deafening was the sound that was altogether absent. Where was the sound of someone who cared about me as I sat on the floor against a wall in a strange hospital while my mother was, hopefully, still struggling to breathe. Where was Chinee and my sisters? To where had they gone and why had they left me. I did not know where to go to even begin looking for them so, I sat...and waited...and hoped...that someone who cared about me would come and find me, soon.

I was to learn later, that a visitor in the hospital had complained rather boisterously that the Niggras sniveling presence was disturbing their confined relative. My siblings had been escorted outside by hospital staff and told to stay there, in the rain, until summoned by one of my Mothers' attendants which did not happen until after she was pronounced dead.

After what felt like hours, but was mere moments, the door opened, and the crash cart was rolled from room number 7. There followed a succession of white shod feet. I never looked up at the faces belonging to those shoes, but one benevolent nurse stopped, came to me, and lifted me to my feet. She bent over as she pulled a handkerchief from her pocket and wiped away tears that I did not realize I was shedding. She told me that my mother had died and that I would be able to see her in a few moments. I made a motion as to move toward the room when she stopped me and gently said that she had to "fix" some things before I could see her, because my Mother's hard-fought battle to live had caused her bodily functions to fail., "Nurse Nice" wanted to make sure my mother was as pretty and fresh as she was when we first arrived. She promised to come and get me when she finished. There were still no signs of my siblings.

"Nurse Nice" eventually returned and took my still throbbing hand in hers as she led me into the darkened room. The overhead lights had been dimmed and only one bedside lamp burned. The venetian blinds had been closed against all but the barest of the early afternoon gloom. Mother lay peacefully upon a bed made with sharply precision corners, the freshly fluffed pillows softly cradled her head. Just a bare hint of a smile softened her face which just moments ago was rigid with the struggle of life. I felt my lungs expanding and collapsing forcefully as I unconsciously willed breath into Mother's unnaturally still body. I genuinely wanted to thank "Nurse Nice" for also being nice to my mother by doing whatever it was she did to "fix" my Mother's bodily function failures, whatever that meant. But all I could do was think how grateful I was that Mother was still as pretty in death as she had been in life and even more grateful that the hideous mask of death of her final moments, which only I witnessed, was not visible upon her face.

As "Nurse Nice" led me from the room, I heard my sisters' voices. I still had not found mine. I looked past them for Chinee. He wasn't there and somewhere deep inside I knew that this time *he* needed me. I walked unsteadily past both sisters, past the nurses' station, and into the parking lot. It had begun to rain now in earnest; it seems that all the Angels in Heavens were weeping along with me. I found Chinee standing with his back to the hospital with his shoulders heaving violently. I'd never seen him cry and did not know how to comfort him. I just walked to him and put one hand in his jacket pocket and put my other arm around his waist and we cried silently together until it was time to leave for home. It broke our hearts to leave Mother in that cold uncaring place but what else could we do? It was a long, silent drive home with one seat in the car, now unoccupied.

Lesson learned? What can possibly be learned from a Mother dying in the arms of her twelve-year-old child, in a hospital where the type of medical care one received depended upon the color of one's skin? When a mob of hate-mongers would keep children from comforting a dying mother or even each other? How did a nurse find the courage and understanding needed to comfort one scared and lost child? Why would she become a crusader of one to save just one, especially in the glare of the disapproving faces of the many? I was the child in that place where it all happened, yet I still ponder how I survived so much pain without complete fracturing, but I am grateful that "Nurse Nice" did not care that she cared and helped me avoid my dark place.

I suppose the lesson should be that regardless of the size of the crowd that offers hate, it's the size of the love given by the one which should always be most memorable. Unfortunately, it often is not. I can still recall the names of my mother's doctor, the two nurses we first encountered and even the names of the two men who kept my mother from receiving lifesaving medical help, but I cannot recall the true name of "Nurse Nice."

MY BROTHER WAS MY KEEPER...

The Funeral, Chinee, and Me

Those first few days following Mother's death happened without any participation at all from me. Most people were generally coming and going without seeing me or pretending not to see me. A smorgasbord of covered dishes took up every flat surface in our kitchen. There was so much food from which to choose yet no one was eating. Cars were parked everywhere around the farm; when one would leave, three others jockeyed for the vacated spot. When food wasn't being brought into the house, alcohol was being slipped in behind it. There were more people going behind the house than coming into it, little wonder since we lived in a dry county, (*no liquor sales*), and alcohol was almost as hard to come by as a paycheck. Music blaring from various car radios reverberated against the heavy, moisture laden spring air. It all felt so disrespectful somehow. The actions of those adults seemed to say to me, "Somebody died? Let's have a Party!" I could not believe that what was happening there on the farm was what a" Wake" was meant to be. As I wandered back and forth around the farm, trying to find a quiet spot in which to think about Mother, people would press money into my hand. Five-, ten-, and twenty-dollar bills. I wanted so desperately to throw it back at them and demand they give me back Mother instead. Why did they think that food, music, or money would clear Mother from my thoughts? I tried several times to tell people how I felt but more often than not, it only produced another five, a pat on the head or murmurs of, "that poor child," trailing behind them as they fled from me. In those moments, I despised them all.

While weaving in and out between parked cars, still looking for an unoccupied spot, I saw sitting beneath one of the two huge Sycamore trees framing our house, my three sisters. A throng of people surrounded them, male and females ready to lend an ear, run and fetch a drink or produce a tissue when tears threatened. But had not I lost my mother too, "where were the shoes to click to my clack? Where was the voice to answer mine back?" I felt truly all alone in the world. I wanted to tell someone what it felt like watching mother die while she crushed my hands with super-human strength. I wanted to ask someone if they thought she was trying to impart something to me or just trying to hold onto the only thing available and familiar in those final moments. I needed to ask anyone, if they thought my mother was in pain during those last minutes because it sure looked as if she was to me or was it her body's natural reaction to a swiftly, catastrophic depletion of oxygen. I wanted to know if the nurse had somehow made Mother look as if she was smiling for my benefit or had Mother's smile been eternally set upon her face because she had caught a glimpse of Heaven and of God's welcoming arms? But most urgently, I needed to know when the nightmares and headaches would stop? I really needed and wanted someone to just hold me or offer a pocket to put my hand into. Where was Chinee?

I did not know where Chinee was. I wanted to believe that he was nearby, but I had not remembered seeing him during those days leading to funeral. Wherever he was, I knew he was hurting even more than I was, because although difficult to believe, Mother and he were even closer than he and I. The concern I held for Chinee's well-being temporarily displaced my own self-centered pain, because I knew he would never openly reveal his pain to anyone, where then would he go to find a willing, sympathetic, and knowing ear? My tears and pain were somewhat abated when finally, I found someone who did not mind sitting with me. Someone who did not try to press money into my palms, whose breath was not soured by cheap liquor. Someone who did not think a pat on the head was a sufficient substitute for a hug. Someone who welcomed me when I curled up next to him on the steps of our back porch and at the moment when I'd reached the pinnacle of misery, unable any longer to keep silent the voice of my pain, allowed his own keen whining to unashamedly match my own...so grateful was I for my little dog Henry.

The funeral had been planned for the 7th, a Sunday, four days after mother died. It's odd how my mind has always played with numbers; Mother was born in the fifth month; she also died in the fifth month in room number 7 and was being buried on the 7th and in 7 days from then, I would spend my first Mother's Day without my mother. Fives and Sevens...I'm reasonably certain that my still compulsive number tracking, which began the day my Mother died, must have a medical or psychological term but as I look back I must simply attribute it to, once again, finding a way to hold onto sanity and keep my dark place vacant.

It was Friday before the funeral and finally someone noticed me, sort of. As everyone was rushing about, laying out, ironing, and pulling together their coordinating outfits for the funeral, I heard my much older cousin Jo, ordering someone to go and grab the outfit which I was to wear. She had offered to freshen it up with the now vacated iron and ironing board. The house had been chaotic for days with people coming and going and so many more coming and staying that a constant low-level buzz had been created, not unlike the sound emanating from a large beehive, even so, all sound ceased immediately after Cousin Jo spoke that one seemingly innocuous request. Someone remembered that I existed and what a stir that memory caused! It had been agreed upon that Mother would be buried in her Eastern Star, Course of Corinthians, Ceremonial white dress. It had also been decided, by whom I wasn't privy, that her daughters would also wear white and Chinee would wear a black suit with a white buttoned-down shirt and black tie. These were the items along with an array of hats, gloves, shoes, purses, and tasteful jewelry which were being pressed, steamed, and matched with mind-numbing monotony. It was then that it occurred to everyone almost at once, that no one had given much thought as to what I would wear. Although everyone, I supposed from snippets I'd overheard afterwards, assumed that I would wear my Easter dress from little more than a month ago however, no one had asked if I had an Easter dress from little more than a month ago, I did not. Mother had been too ill to go shopping for a dress for me so, after putting on what I thought to be my grownup face, I determined to put Mother at ease by declaring that I neither needed nor wanted a new dress. She had smiled knowingly, caressed my cheek, and thanked me for being so understanding and wise beyond my years; she promised to make it up to me when she felt better, she never did...feel better.

The problem I had created by having the audacity to not have a suitable outfit to wear to Mother's funeral was unforgivable, if the look etched on the faces in that room was of any measure. "Well, there's nothing to do," someone declared, "except to go and find something for her to wear." It was near 10 a.m. Friday morning and I was quietly rejoicing that I was at least for the time being, the center of attention, but something deep within me warned against showing any joy at this turn of events, especially when I heard someone murmur, "Those girls have enough on their minds without having to go shopping for her". *HER?* Wasn't...I...one...of...those...girls...too?

(There was no grouping of nouns, verbs, adverbs, or adjectives which could have made me feel less important or more distant from my family than those just uttered).

My three sisters, Cousin Jo, and I piled into an available car and drove first to the closest town, Newton, about 15 miles away to the south. It was thought that since we were in the midst of spring with the promise of summer approaching, it would be an easy matter to find a simple white dress. Newton was fresh out. We then headed for Jasper, approximately 16-mile northwest of Newton. We were sure this twice as large city would have at least several choices from which to choose. It did not. If I had any joy remaining from being the center of attention, it disappeared somewhere between the trip in and out of Jasper's last department store and I had fervently begun to wish to be forgotten again, swiftly. With no other shops within fifty miles, it was determined that we'd return home and sift through my things to see if something could be thrown together. Now, I was crestfallen, not only would I not appear as part of a white clad grieving family unit, but I was being relegated to a poor relation of the white clad family unit; someone to be thrown together then thrown aside. Oh well, at least I'd gotten my wish; I was no longer the center of attention.

Cousin Jo, older than Mother by at least 3 years, saw through my thin veneer of bravery and announced that I would be accompanying her on the sixty miles trip back to her Beaumont home that evening and there, we'd go shopping for a dress on Saturday. My second eldest sister demurred that this was too much trouble and wasn't necessary. Gratefully, Cousin Jo placed her hand on her wide hips, tilted her head to one side, and with a blistering gaze aimed unswervingly at that same sister, declared that she was not asking permission and thus clearly ending the conversation. (Beaumont, during this time, was second only to Houston as far as a shopping venue, in closer proximity to our home and being so, all concerns of finding an appropriate white dress in my size was allayed and I could be soon forgotten, again. It is difficult to imagine that the entire retail populous of East Texas could pull off such a detailed conspiracy in a mere thirty-six-hour span, but it did, clearly, it did).

After going in and out of so many shops and trying on untold numbers of too long, too short, too mature, and too frilly dresses, it was I who finally surrendered and begged to quit. My plea was hardly necessary since we had exhausted all options. Walking back to the car, Cousin Jo remembered that her youngest daughter had an as yet unworn, new suit which would fit me perfectly, it did; and that it would surely be the perfect outfit for the funeral tomorrow. It wasn't. Though very tasteful and the most grown-up outfit I'd ever worn, it was not white by a long shot; not even in the white family, well not all of it anyway. It was a three-piece olive-green suit with matching skirt and jacket, cream piping, and a cream camisole. I was too tired to care and decided that it made no difference anyway. It would not bring mother back. But there was something about that suit of which my mind strained toward a memory, but it could not quite grasp. Whatever it was, brought with it a shiver of fear and I gladly set it aside.

Sadly, Sunday morning arrived, and I had been dressed, coifed, and threatened with bodily harm by second eldest, that if one spot appeared on the borrowed outfit, if a hair on my head was moved out of place, or even if the tiniest run appeared in the nylons which searched for a place to cling to my pencil thin legs. No one, she warned me, would take the time to put me back together if I became careless and so thoughtless as to undo myself. I declined breakfast, fearful of a drip of jelly, or a dropped forkful of egg, only to be harangued by my other sisters who were telling me to eat because it would be hours before the opportunity presented itself again. I chose instead to sit in a chair on the front porch and to continue looking for Chinee in the horde of people who kept suddenly appearing from no place. I'd had no interaction with Chinee since we had arrived home from the hospital on Wednesday, although I continued to sense him nearby. I found out much later that Chinee was going through the most intensely emotional and painful time of his life. I was only too aware of his and mother's deep affection for each other so I could only surmise how much he needed me and how I, steeped in my own despair, had failed him. I vowed a childishly resolute pledge that I would never again let him down in his hour of need no matter what he may ask of me. Years later, I would come to lament this unspoken vow, but I never willingly broke it.

The family's limousine arrived from the mortuary and all my sisters, a few of my Mother's friends, and Chinee all climbed solemnly inside. I stood there waiting for my turn to enter but I was pushed aside as the door was closed by one of the attendants. (I guess he could not tell that I was part of the family, since I wasn't wearing white). Just as I finished forming that thought, the door opened suddenly and I heard someone (a family friend/distant relative) from inside say, "Aw now, she can ride with Roscoe, close the door." Chinee said, "she'll ride in here with us or we all will damn well walk!" With that, he leaned out, grabbed me by my arm and pulled me inside. We drove the nineteen miles to Jasper in relative silence to accompany the hearse which would carry my Mother's body back to Shankleville's Mount Hope Missionary Baptist Church, with me riding in the only comfortable seat in that limousine, Chinee's lap.

Chinee and I were separated when we arrived at the church and though I had been permitted to ride in the limo, albeit reluctantly, I would not be allowed to sit with my family inside the church. The front row pew to the left of the church had been reserved for the most immediate family members, or should I say the adult immediately family members and the necessary minions appointed to hug, hold, fan, and comfort my sisters and brother. I had been banished to a pew three rows back and forced to sit with an aunt-in-law, who admittedly disliked my mother and obviously cared just a bit less for all but one of Mother's children, I wasn't that One. Throughout the service, I strained my neck to peer into the casket that held my Mother. Back then, the casket was routinely kept open throughout the service. Family members and friends could approach the casket to bid their final farewells at the end of the service. I was afraid that since I was not on the front row, I would not be given an opportunity to take a last look at my mother.

Each of my searching strains were answered by a vicious, twisting, and violent pinch, apparently gleefully administered by my aunt-in-law, all while I was being told to sit still. There were tears streaming from the eyes of my sibling but none of theirs tears were tinged with the physical pain that accompanied mine. I longed for both my brother and my mother.

Somehow, the memorial service ended, and my bruised arm and I found ourselves standing next to Mother's casket. She looked just as she had when last, I'd seen her at the hospital; the little smile still on her face brought a small, a very small measure of comfort to me. Too soon, we were all ushered back into the various automobiles and ordered to follow the hearse. At the gravesite, once again, there was seating only for four. I stood across from my siblings with the yawning grave separating us. I stood at the very periphery of that gaping, anticipating aperture which was to be Mother's final earthly resting place.

I heard the minister reading the verses leading to interment and it was not that I was purposely trying to ignore what he was saying but there was a sound coming from the grave, a gurgling!

I dared a quick look around to see if anyone else had picked up on the sound. But I must have moved too quickly because my movement was met with another blood-clotting pinch by that same Aunt, from which darkest part of Hell had she come? As Minister Lockett exhorted us to take to heart the passage of which he was about to read, something niggled at my consciousness and as he began to recite the Scripture's chapter and verse, the gurgling, bubbling sound grew louder and became a crescendo of thunder ushering in an unwanted, uninvited dream I did not want to remember. "Children," said Minister Lockett, "Christ has left us a road of which if we follow, we will find not only Him at the end of it but our loved ones as well. Your mother has not left you no more than Christ has left us. He went to prepare a place for us and your Mother is now occupying her place in God's kingdom and she will be waiting for you when God calls your name...St. John 14th Chapter...", it was then in that moment that I lost the ability to breathe. The forgotten dream came flooding back, filling me with unexplained yet experienced dread. I recalled crying in that dream because I did not have a white dress. I remembered mother lying in a white casket wearing a white dress. I remembered a grave dug above an underground spring, filling slowly, slowly, slowly with water...I remembered...nothing else because gratefully my brain turned off the switch that kept me upright and supposedly I went down, muddying the borrowed outfit, sending every strand of hair on my head astray, and snagging the new nylons as I went. Although it was later blamed on my ill-fated decision not to eat breakfast, I knew better and so would have Mother, if she was not already seated around God's throne.

My Brother Was My Keeper...
Fair Warning

This next chapter is written with a fair share of angst; not because my truth has wavered but indeed because it has not. So far each chapter has centered upon people who impacted my life but who have traveled beyond this sphere in preparation of receiving whatever rewards they earned while here.

The upcoming chapter will also include individuals who no longer walk among us but have left behind some whom I trust cared & loved them. With this in mind and before I go further, I declare openly that as an adult, I have never intentionally administered hatred or meanness of spirit toward anyone and it is not my intentions to do so here. Admittedly, I will acknowledge the words contained in the next chapter could affect those who will recognize and still mourn the ones of whom I will write, but unfortunately none of us exist in a bubble or in exclusivities. We are like the concentric lines created when one drops a pebble into still water, expanding further and further until the pebble is forgotten but the effect lives on. We, each one of us, touch others either positively or negatively, some deliver both equally.

There might be those of you reading this who think it unfair of me to write of people who are no longer here to defend themselves. Suffice to say, that each person of whom I've documented as having negatively impacted "my" life had years and some had decades in which to make a defense but chose not, that is, all but one and to that One, I offered my genuine respect and earnest forgiveness for him having done so. For these others, I offer long calculated forgiveness and the promise to live in truth and surprisingly, a minute measure of gratitude.

These of whom I have written and some of whom I will write, used cruel and brutish behavior against me and thereby changed who I was meant to be. That being said,, I am not altogether unhappy with the person I have become because the person I became, despises cruelty in any form toward any group but especially children. Because of some of whom I will write, I support the absolute right of others to exist without fear of physical or emotional abuse or degradation. I have found I am most at ease with those who were similarly treated but did not take as long as I did to find the road to forgiveness. I admire those who managed to move forward, unbroken, without sweet memories to sustain them in the worst of times. I am continually grateful that the ills imposed upon me did not everlastingly disturb my equanimity.

Because those who used their words to assist them in administering their various means of physical torture upon my person, I am acutely aware of the harm words can induce, therefore I avoid, obsessively so, any situations or occurrences whereby I might be called upon to apologize. Apologies do not spring forth easily from me.

It is for the reasons I have mentioned above that I am forewarning, not apologizing, for this next chapter chronicling a decisive time in my life. I attempted to articulate at the onset of this journey that I would write without embellishments with compelling honesty. Therefore, if my life and what was done to me in my life offends anyone who may recognize their loved ones within these pages or hold memories opposing mine, I challenge you to hold tightly to those memories. In no way do I wish to take them from you or change them; on the contrary, your good memories indicate that there dwelled redeeming qualities within your loved ones even though they chose to keep those qualities from me.

I hope with utmost sincerity that there appears to be no bitterness seeping from my fingertips and staining these pages because, truly, I am not bitter, although I could make compelling arguments as to why I should be. Complete truth has sharp edges, but it generally only lends its blade against those who attempt to use it under the cloak darkness. Wielding a knife in darkness is a dangerous affair therefore, I live in the light and anything I have done in coarseness has only injured me. In some baffling and astounding way, I am grateful to each person who chose to deliver abject cruelty upon me as a defenseless child. But in moments of quiet reflections, of which I have had many, their hateful voices come uncompelled, and my soul flinches as each remembered lash cuts through the years, and leave its mark, this time upon my heart instead of my back. It is during those times when I wonder, if not for those who inflicted their best, who I might have become, what different road I might have traveled. Would I have eventually found myself yet in the same place, howbeit by a different route? I wonder.

Throughout the passing years, I have often been asked by relatives and friends, why it was that I left home and more importantly to them, why I left in the manner I did. I always avoided the truth of the matter and found unfulfilling ways to sidestep their probing inquiries. I will, however, finally address those questions.

To those whose memories of your loved ones differ from mine, despite what will be disclosed herein, I hope those memories will continue to bring you comfort as you live within your own truth or within the parameters of theirs.

As I contemplate the next chapter, please consider the hauntingly beautiful and appropriate words of William Wordsworth,

"*What though the radiance which was once so bright be now forever taken from my sight. Though nothing can bring back the hour of splendor in the grass, of glory in the flower. We will grieve not, rather find strength in what remains behind. In the primal sympathy, which having been must ever be. In the soothing thoughts that spring out of human sufferings; In the faith that looks through death, in years that bring the philosophic mind.*"

My Brother Was My Keeper...
The Escape, Chinee, and Me

The days passed quickly after the funeral and my emotions were still running close to the surface. Most of the out-of-town relatives and friends had left or were leaving our home to resume the lives they had put on hold for the past week. My two uncles and their families were among the last to leave. Also, last to leave were my two eldest sisters who were being given a lift back to Houston so as not to miss to their flight back to Los Angeles.

Even as the luggage was being placed into the cars, no one had yet spoken to me as to what was to become of me. I determined therefore, that I did not need any of them. I would simply remain in the family home with Papa and we would take care of each other. Quite an undertaking for a slight, 12-year-old girl and an 85-year-old, feeble gentleman, however, the overwhelming improbability of my thought did not concern me, at least for the few brief moments in which I entertained the idea.

During the morning of my Mother's funeral, my Papa who had lost his much-adored only daughter, was now being dealt even more heartbreaking news. My Uncle, standing his full height looking down at his father, told him that he would not be able to attend Mother's funeral because of his frailty. An icy chill, which had nothing to do with the early Spring weather, enveloped the room. As I stood on the right side of Papa's bed and my uncle's great physical presence filled the space on the left, I took hold of Papa's hand and watched as his face clouded over first with anger and then defiance. Those same two characteristics which had prompted him to accept no slight or injury, aimed at himself or anyone he loved, ever. The strength of his own self-worth and the proud carriage which had propelled him even in his declining years, informed anyone who encountered him, that he would brook no disrespect in any form. Papa's unmovable stance in life and his distinctive personality was his unspoken sentence that his will would not be questioned and his ever present 12-gauge, double barreled shotgun, served as the exclamation point.

The anger and defiance which had flickered across Papa's face slowly collapsed as he began to accept the inevitability of his son's proclamation. Until this very point in his life, he had never allowed anyone to impose their will upon him, at least, not without a fight. Mother had always used gentle persuasion and allowed him an opportunity to express his desires, even though they both knew that he would eventually acquiesce to her suggestions. My heart crumbled as he accepted defeat; and those damnable tears began to slip from his eyes, something again, I had never witnessed and had difficulty knowing what to do with this new emotional pain layered upon all the other new pains. There was no way to know if Papa's tears were shed because of the realization he no longer held the authoritarian position as the Head of his family or because he could not, rather would not, be allowed to go before his daughter's coffin and escort her to her final resting place, as was his right.

My tears had no choice other than to match Papa's and there were not enough handkerchiefs to be found on the whole of our farm to dry our collective tears. Papa looked away from his son, covered my hand with his and gently pulled me down onto the bed with him as he had so many times throughout the years as nightmares or headaches had chased me from my bed to the safety of his and my grandmother's. I put my head on his once proud but now bowed in defeat shoulders and there he offered comfort to me as he stroked my head and told me how I needed to begin to prepare to live life without him as well. I was further aggrieved as he told me things that I was not ready to hear or accept. He told me of hurtful things he had suffered at the hands of others early in his life. I knew, without asking, that some of what he had share with me that day, had been never shared with anyone else and I have never repeated what he told me, but I have tried to honor it with every breath I have taken since. It is impossible to know how long we laid there, exchanging no additional words, but commiserating with each other in despair. It could have been five minutes or sixty, it did not matter because each tick of the small clock perched on the shelf above his bed, brought pain afresh with no promise of it easing with the passage of time.

Papa had reluctantly but completely surrendered hours later, when he had made his mark upon papers turning over the care of the farm and of himself to his son. I do not believe Papa had ever faced such profuse sadness, but there would soon be one more heartbreak he would have to face. However, that heartbreak would give rise to him once again, though briefly, regaining his place as the decision maker and guardian of those he loved best. I'm proud to say, I was now first on his short list of those he loved best.

There was only one car left in the driveway Monday afternoon and there had still not been a single, "Don't worry, we have made sure that you will be ok," given to me. Not one, "We are going to take care of you," nor was there a, "We will call every now and again to see how you are doing." Perhaps they thought it was none of my concern. How could such a fractured soul ever become whole again after so many blatantly uncaring acts by adults?

Chinee had gone away again, and I suspected that he was finding it more than a little difficult making his way without Mother. He was wandering here and there and sleeping wherever he happened to be when darkness fell. Further delaying his healing was the lingering and deep resentment he harbored toward one of Mother's "supposed" friends, whom he thought had bullied her way into our home, not only making unreasonable demands but, confiscating Mothers' personal items and clothing, not only for herself but for certain of her grandchildren as well. She had shown no concern as to the desires or wishes of Mothers' children, regarding her once treasured but now left behind belongings. The one which angered Chinee most, was the taking of one of Mother's beloved possessions; a beautiful, winter weigh, heavily lined, full length, white leather coat which Chinee had worked several summers trimming overhanging trees for the Roads Department, in order to make it a gift to her. Mother had gone winter after winter without a proper outer garment to protect her from our frigid weather and Chinee had proudly handed her the money he had earned and exacted a promise from her that she would spend it only on a warm coat. She did. Now, that too was gone, taken by The Woman.

So, for Chinee, this began a pattern that was to remain the entire length of this life. Whenever something bothered or hurt him too deeply, he simply moved away from the source of his pain, far away. It was not in his nature to purposely cause pain, although his intimidating size often suggested otherwise. He would rather subject himself to pain than to hurt others.

(This was the reason he had not flattened Mrs. Brown when he'd had the opportunity).

Chinee would have had to feel he had been backed into a corner before he would even raise his voice in anger and if he did, people would scatter. Chinee's control of his rage was so tightly managed that people often mistook his "walk away nature" as a weakness, little did they know.

And so now, there was just me and Papa and of course, Mother's friend, "The Woman." I still could not figure out why she was there, and more importantly how and when was she going to leave. She did not drive and consequently had no automobile. Everyone she could have possibly ridden home with had already left. Of all the people who could have been accidently left behind, why had this ONE Woman missed her ride? She was 5 feet nothing else and had to be weighed on a grain scale. She was a large woman with a temper which competed with her heft. I was trying to think of a tactful way in which to ask how she was going to get home, when my process was interrupted by her thunderous command, to go and bring her overnight bag in from the porch. I knew my feet did not move right away because I was not sure that I had heard correctly. Did not "overnight" suggest that something or someone would remain where something or someone was until at least daybreak the following day? I was not given an opportunity to ponder further because for what she deemed to be insolent behavior on my part, she delivered a half-closed fist to my forehead. Stunned, both physically and emotionally, I stumble and fell hard against the kitchen table. That stumble had injured a rib; one which was never treated and took ages to heal. Even though her extraordinary size deceptively made one think she was slow moving, she had suddenly appeared as if she was everywhere at once. "If you don't get your lazy, good for nothing ass out there and do what I tell you now, you'll wish they buried you with your mama, now git gal!"

I'd half crouched, and half ran the few remaining steps to the back porch and wonders upon wonders, there it was, a brown overnight case. Why had not I seen it before? I struggled with the weight of the case because my head was still reeling, and my painful rib limited my movement. I sat it down on the floor next to her and quickly stepped away from her immediate reach. I heard Papa calling to me and I hurried to his bedside, tears and snot mingling together. Papa had heard everything; worry and concern creased his face. Storm clouds brewed behind his still clear, greenish brown eyes. Although an invalid now, when healthy, Papa would have killed anyone who had even entertained a thought of harming someone he loved and there was not one person within a hundred-mile radius who would have questioned the veracity of this statement. However, here all alone with a bewildered orphan, he was only able to commiserate the sadness of our poor lot.

It had been my uncles and sisters who had conspired to have The Woman move in and care for Papa five days a week. She would return home and someone else would do weekend duty for Papa. It was not a mistake that I said she was to care for Papa. I was, in her opinion, an unfortunate and, as yet, uncompensated for inconvenience which had to be tolerated, at least that was what she told me fairly often, almost daily. "Since I have to cook for Daddy Bob, I guess I can leave enough scrapings in the pot to feed you."

So began my life after the funeral. I was excitedly looking forward to the first weekend Papa and I would have alone or at least without her. Imagine my stunned surprise when that first happily, anticipated Friday evening arrived, and she told me to get a paper bag and put a dress and two pair of underwear in it. "I'll be damned if I'm leaving you up here in these woods to gap your legs open to any Tom's Harry Dick! (Wasn't that supposed to be Tom, Dick, and Harry)? "Hell," she said, "I'm already saddled with you, and I'll be gawd-dammed if I take care of another snot-nose bastard!"

Please believe me as I write that I had not an inkling as to what she was alluding. Mother had only one opportunity to

84

briefly and not completely explain to me a few of the facts of life, and that was a mere four months before she'd died, and only after my first uninvited but supposedly welcomed monthly visitor arrived. Even then, she had only told me that I had "become a Missy" and would have to limit my tree climbing, my football playing, my wrestling and almost every other fun thing in life. I did not understand that "Missy" business at all, unless it meant "missing out." She had showed me the necessary techniques to protect my clothing, how to clean myself, and how to clean my clothing if an accident should happen. She said that we would talk more later, we never did. Therefore, I was completely unaware of The Woman's implications.

I was to accompany The Woman to her home every weekend! I felt trapped in ways that would be impossible to explain if these pages numbered in the thousands. No more lazy weekends running with my puppy, Henry. No more searching for hidden treasures in the woods surrounding the farm. No more lying on the ground and finding animals in the clouds, gone, all buried with Mother.

Since I was an undesired part of this woman's life, she had decided that I would at least earn my keep. So, I scrubbed, I ironed, and I fed chickens, (Those terrifying creatures whose only place in life should be in flour, hot oil and only afterwards, on the Sunday table); and I hung clothes and folded linen. I gathered wood and stacked it. I ran errands to nearby neighbors and collected needed items from, a somewhat nearby, grocer. I was so exhausted by the end of that first Saturday evening; I had only enough energy remaining to be grateful that I was allowed a cot on which to sleep. I could not fathom why nothing I did ever suited this woman. Each job I accomplished fell short of her expectations, and I was severely dealt with because of it. I was never made aware of the mistakes beforehand; they were only made apparent as I walked past her to do the next chore. She would grab me from behind and slap me with hands that were made more forceful by the sheer weight of them. She would beat me with extension cords, telephone receivers, or a broom handle, if I happened to be beyond her natural reach. There was even a time when the only thing within her reach was a Sunbeam iron. It took weeks before the ringing in my ear subsided. I am profoundly grateful that it had not been turned on and heated. Still, I never stopped trying to please her, if for no other reason than to limit the abuse.

I eventually came to understand this woman's unwarranted, unnecessary, and extremely crude explanation of why she would not leave me on the farm with Papa. However, she should have considered the supreme lack of wisdom she displayed in leaving me in her home, alone and unprotected with her 18-year-old grandson.

Since the punishment she had administered with the electric iron some weeks before, I stood ever ready and taut with anxiety when called upon to do her bidding. I was elated when I would accomplish two tasks in a row without some type of berating either physical or emotional. She had begun what had become almost a mantra by telling me daily that I was so damn ugly that if any man was ever so old, so blind, or so desperate as to ask me to marry him,, I should accept his proposal without delay because it would be my only opportunity to find a man willing to tie his lot to mine. Of course, I believed her, why wouldn't I, adults did not lie to children, did they? The woman, who by the end of July having been wholly successful in her campaign to instill unwavering fear in me, began to leave me at her house instead of dragging me along with her to the different communities and summer events, called Homecomings.

Homecomings, as the name suggest, were and still are, annual celebrations held in conjunction with community Churches, whereby current and former members of said communities would come together and celebrate, History, Heritage, and Family. There were no restrictions placed upon who could or could not attend any Homecoming. Many of the same local people would attend the Homecomings in communities other than their own in anticipation of seeing and visiting with returning, former citizens. From its earliest inception and throughout the late 1960's and 1980's, these wonderful events encompassed a complete weekend. Friday nights were generally set aside for traveling and soul stirring gospel trios and quartets. Saturday evening celebrations concentrated upon the performances of local and visiting church choirs. The weekend would culminate with fire and fiery sermons and the all-important, excitedly discussed, much ballyhooed, open air picnic where each family's matriarch would put on display her best dishes. Although none of the women would ever admit to it, the competition was fierce, but the hungry children were the winners in all the competitions, because everyone was too willing to share the contents of their "pans" with each passing child.

This next section was written not to shock but again, for the truth of the matter. I could have elected to leave it out altogether and no one, other than me, would have been the wiser. However, this experience had every bit as much to do with shaping who I was to become, perhaps even more, than any of the other preceding life changing events I've chronicled here. I refuse to believe that what I reveal here only happened once or that it only happened to me. It could not have, because sick and abysmal behavior does not cease to exist just because we wish it to, nor does it stop if its presence is not brought to awareness but rather kept hidden away. With the writing of this chapter, I release any remaining shreds of guilt that I placed, or more correctly, was placed upon me by the offender. The offender left this life before I had found the opportunity to place the guilt directly back upon him, where it belonged, by making the offense known. Therefore, for years, I carried it alone! Perhaps the burning, white-hot coals of contempt that was forced upon me is now being pressed upon him in the hell the Afterlife holds for him. Whereby, the base part of my being, would dearly love to take some measure of pleasure in that consideration. I admit that I do pray that perhaps at some point before that miserable excuse of humanity escaped life here, he sought and found God's forgiveness through His Mercy and Grace. I further pray, that if other victims of this Tool of Satan somehow happen upon these pages, they too will find the strength to remove the horrendous twins of unwarranted guilt and shame from their shoulders and put it squarely on this offender where, even in death, it belongs.

It was during one of those Friday night Homecoming events when the woman left me in the care of her grandson. He had not been in the house when she had left, and I had lain across my bed, a little cot in a room directly off the enclosed front porch, and began one of my favorite pastimes, reading. I did not hear him enter the small room, but some sense alerted me to another's presence, and I looked over my shoulder and saw him standing there. I relayed the message the woman instructed me to give him and went back to my book. I had not heard him leave and thought perhaps he had not heard what I had said. I was about to repeat the message when I heard movement, glanced over my shoulder, and saw him lunge towards the bed. Thanks to the recent lessons taught me by his grandmother, I instinctively shank from him and thereby prevented him and his, at a minimal, hundred and fifty-pound weight advantage from pinning me directly beneath him. The situation confused me but had not yet frightened me because he had been a sympathetic, albeit silent, witness to the cruel treatment I received from his grandmother, The Woman. I sat fully up; my book momentarily forgotten. I was about to ask what he was doing when he grabbed my shoulders and pushed me back onto the mattress tearing a page of my book! Now, I was just angry! I told him to get his hands off me and to leave me alone. He did not and the look on his face said that he had no intentions of doing so. That was when I became frightened. Although there was another house about 100 yards or so away, there were no lights on indicating there might be someone there to help if my screams were heard. He still had not spoken a word to me, just kept pushing me down and pulling at my clothes and I kept trying to squirm away, not understanding his intentions and not liking his actions. The ever hardening look on his face and the constant tugging on my clothes had now ignited a fight or flight urgency. Fleeing was not yet an option so I began kicking out at any part of his body I could reach. I must have hit a pocket of soft tissue some place because he grunted, grabbed himself, and rolled away for about a five count! I looked for a quick escape from the little room which boasted two doors, one leading directly to the front porch and freedom and the other leading back through a connecting bedroom, then the sitting room and then onto the front porch. I needn't have bothered looking for an exit because his hulk blocked both exits at once. I scooted as far back as I could into the corner of the bed and was ready to strike out again when he finally spoke and frightened me more than I had been since I was five!

As he spoke, I could feel my body shivering from panic! He smiled but there was no mirth or warmth to it as he informed me that his grandmother, he used his familiar name for her, knew what he was doing and in fact, had given him permission! He went on to say that he could hardly wait until she returned so that he could tell her of my misbehavior! There was nothing that he could have said or done that would have terrified me more. He knew his threats and measured words had found their intended mark when he saw the tears, those freaking, damnable betraying tears! He laughed aloud when I begged him to not tell his grandmother! My humiliation was complete, and fear so overwhelmed me that I begged him to do whatever he wanted to do to me, only please, just don't tell that I had fought him! I begged him to accept that I did not understand and that I would not fight him again, but he just backed out of the room laughing even louder and taunting me even more.

I stayed huddled in that corner too afraid to move and too afraid to sleep. I wanted to go home but it was as dark as pitch outside and the farm was five miles away. My life was over I decided. She would certainly kill me tonight and have me buried somewhere on the property. I wanted so badly to be rescued from this hell, I wanted even more for him to come back and give me another chance to behave correctly, even though I did not know what that would entail. I pondered what there was about me, that made me the brunt of so much maltreatment from so many adults. Why, God? I was still sitting in that corner rocking myself when The Woman returned home. I was still sitting there rocking when night gave way to daybreak. I was beyond caring when she yelled to me to come and empty her chamber pot. I stumble through Saturday and Sunday, not eating, not drinking, only wanting her to begin the beating and get it over. Sometime late Sunday afternoon as we waited on the ride that would take us back to the farm, she had finally noticed my lethargy and decided that I must be physically ill and forced me to swallow her cure-all, 2 tablespoons of Castor oil! Why, God...Why?

It was months later when I realized that he had lied to me. The Woman knew nothing of his attempts on my person. It was several years later when I finally had a name for what he had meant to do to me. When that realization came, I loathed him with a contempt reserved for only the vilest among us and it would not be contained easily. Something changed within my core at that moment of realization! Whatever mentality my DNA

structure had demanded, had now, because of the evil machina-
tions of evil personalities, AT THAT MOMENT, became inex-
orably altered.

Not only had he attempted to rape me, not only had he made
sport of my debilitating fear of The Woman, but he had laughed
and sneered derisively at me when I unknowingly begged him,
my intended rapist, to continue the act because my fear of being
beaten was to me, I believed, worse than anything he could do.
My hatred did not grow from the attempt, my hatred grew, and
I still struggle to keep its incessant gnawing at bay, because he
forced me to unknowingly beg him to rape me because of the
fear his grandmother had beaten into me. *He...goaded...me...
into...begging...him...to...rape...me He...then...laughed...at...my...
renewed...pain... and...disappointment...*

as...he...refused...my...pleas!

Gratefully, I saw him no more that summer. Someone said
he had returned to live with his immediate family. However, I
did have reason to occupy the same time and space with him
eleven years later, when he no longer held any threat to my mind
or body. I had purposely displaced several people as I wran-
gled a seat directly opposite of him whereby he had no choice
other than to look into my staring, accusing eyes each time he
looked up and each time he did, he would too quickly look away,
betraying his guilt. Even as the time of that occurrence drew to a
close, I hurried to be the first to exit the building. My intentions
were to wait for him at the bottom of the steps as he exited and
force a confrontation. He saw me too soon and cowardly took
another route out of the building. It did not end there. At the
next location, as he sat, I stood opposite of him, willing him to
look up and across the six feet or so that separated us, six feet
and a coffin. Because of his increased girth, his agility surprised
me, as he again, at the conclusion, used the crowd to cover his
swift exit. I wanted to humiliate him, and it had not mattered to

me that he was there to attend to the burial of his father because I was there to attend to the burial of my Uncle, his father, his grandmother's, The Woman's son-in-law.

For years, I indulged in a sad preoccupation of rapist and their victims. Not a fascination entailing the disgusting acts they committed but of their ability to control their victims through fear, intimidation, shame, and guilt, which admittedly is equally disgusting. Through my amateur research, I discovered that back on that summer night, in that little bedroom directly off The Woman's front porch, as I had fought to defend myself, that the pitiful act of my pleading with him to complete the attack upon my person, is what saved me. I had given him power by means of my fear but my willingness to capitulate stripped him of whatever excitement he had gained by intimidation. Understanding my attacker's mentality was the first step toward defeating him mentally. He remained until the day he died a miserable death, in a miserable manner, a miserable person. His immediate family desirous of it or not, has my sympathy. His other victims have my support.

When I began this journey, it was not to expose anyone's faults or shortcomings. It was, however, my attempt to exorcise the demons other people's shortcomings injected into my life.

Over the years when I did allow a few people glimpses into my childhood, I was often told things along the lines of, "you're a strong person." Those statements were always met with a fair amount of denial, self-deprecation, and in some cases outright cynicism. I was never strong; I was a person without a choice. What I was, was a person looking for a soft, private place to have a complete breakdown. Since I am very defining in my choices, it took many years for me to find the perfect place for that complete breakdown.

When one of my sons was a "just learning to toddle" toddler, he would hold onto the edges of my sofa and work his way around to the back of it. Once there, he would look back and assuring himself that he had found a place of privacy, (he never looked up or he would have seen me peering over the top of the sofa), his beautiful little face would scrunch up in a knot of solid concentration. His cheeks would puff out and his perfect lips would form the sweetest pout as he would push and push until his diaper was sufficiently tested against leakages. He would then reverse his trip and with the biggest smile and a look of proud completion. He would toddle over to me and offer me his diaper full of crap to unload! Hah! Well, he was my example as I looked for a private place to unload my crap! Just as he had no way of knowing he was being watched, I certainly never expected anyone other than those closest to me to witness my unloading and certainly never assumed that hundreds upon hundreds upon hundreds would witness my trip behind my sofa.

These chapters have provided me that perfect place for my breakdown or perhaps my breakthrough.

The anger that once roiled and propelled me through life has been stamped down. The bitterness of the bile that I was forced to constantly swallow has lost its flavor. Although I cannot say that I am free from all of the negative effects of others, I can say that I am no longer guided by them.

I am constrained to admit that despite the unconscionable, unreasonable, and intemperate abuse, both physical and emotional, heaped upon me by The Woman, she treated my grandfather, with the utmost care and concern. Regardless as to whether her benevolence resulted from a hidden knob of virtue or a highly perceptible fear of my Uncles, I'm grateful to her for her kind treatment of my Papa.

I flatly refused to return to school following Mother's funeral. I had simply lost all desire or compunction to attend and neither the threat of, nor an actual beating was enough to sway my decision. There had only been about 3 weeks remaining in the school year when Mother died, and nobody truly insisted upon my return anyway.

August 1967 was the beginning of the new school year and still I refused to return to school. The melancholy, the depression, sense of hopelessness, and the fear of being pitied were just too deeply ingrained for me to ignore. It was not until the "Girl's" Principal, pushed beyond a reasonable waiting period, decided to leave the school and drive to the farm. She did not sweetly request my return. She did not threaten me, nor did she coddle me. She walked into my home, one hand on her hip, bowed legs planted firmly, and told me without preamble to go and get properly dressed for school and to do so quickly. Mrs. C. was the embodiment of morality and held deep concern for the students in her care. Without discussion, I did as I was told and within ten minutes, we were on the road headed to school. For a passing moment, I contemplated confiding in her my plight but thought better of it. She lived in the same county, but her home was about 40 miles away, therefore she rented rooms from The Woman during the school week. Their relationship, although built on business, was still too close to chance speaking up. It was another decisive life moment.

On the drive to school, she told me of a conversation she'd had with Mother. I had trouble at first following what she was saying because I was shaken by the knowledge that she had actually spoken with Mother and that thought in turn led me to wondering when that conversation might have taken place. It was altogether possible that she had said when the conversation had taken place but ruminating so entirely on her opening declaration, I missed it if indeed she had.

Rousing from my reverie, I heard her repeat something Mother had often said. I had absolutely no doubt that Mrs. C. had spoken with Mother when she said, "Your Mama told me that her last wish was that at least one of her children completes and graduates from school." She continued by saying, "You are the youngest, therefore her last wish and hope rest entirely upon your shoulders."

I fought to control the crushing loneliness and grief which had begun to engulf me again as I remembered Mother saying those very words many times over the years. Those words had never really depended so completely upon me as they did at that vital moment. If this was, and I knew that it was, so important to Mother that in her final weeks, she had sought an ally to help fulfill her dream, then I would have to do my utmost to make her dream a reality. It was little enough to have asked.

My march back into that school, that dear old island of maroon and gold, was accompanied by a dauntless determination and so, I left behind the dread which had escorted and entered her car with me.

A few weeks after I'd returned to school, I had been subjected to a particularly unconscionably, brutish beating with an electrical extension cord. The woman had been careful, or so she had thought, to do her worse to me out of the range of Papa's hearing. This was made easier for her to accomplish because Papa's hearing had been almost totally compromised and because I had become resolute in my refusal to cry out no matter the severity of the attacks. I felt it was my responsibility to not cause Papa additional agony because of his inability to protect me by not letting him hear me cry out in pain.

Looking back and considering those thrashings through the lens of time, I suppose I could have limited the length of the beating had I simply cried out and sated her desire to inflict pain. Instead, I endured until her enormous arms grew fatigued and the torture ceased.

That latest lashing ripped open the skin on my back in multiple long strips and left me crumpled on our back porch, almost unconscious. I believe she would have been content to leave me there all night had she not needed me to bring in her damnable and deplorable chamber pot.

After the pain subsided enough to allow me to walk without stumbling, under the secrecy of darkness, I'd made my way the hundred or so yards to my Mother's cottage and looked for anything to treat my bleeding and throbbing back. Strewn on the floor were a few of the possessions least wanted by the vultures and had been left behind. I found a box containing several Modess sanitary pads, an almost empty container of Bactine antiseptic spray, and an Ace bandage Mother had used on her injured knee. I dribbled the contents of the Bactine down my back as much as the pain allowed, placed the pads on the floor atop the Ace bandage, laid myself on top of them both and wrapped my back the best I could. The tightness of the bandage and the pads contained the bleeding, just as they had been designed, albeit for different reasons, they worked.

Unfortunately, that one application of antiseptic was not enough to stifle the incident of infection. The severity of my wounds conspired with the overwhelming East Texas August heat and biting flies. The flies having found an easy host upon which to both feed and lay their eggs created a flaming, odorous, oozing infection from which I could find no relief.

For reasons unknown to me, The Woman decided to leave me at the farm the second Friday following that vicious beating. Perhaps she did not want my ruptured back soiling her linens, but upon awakening at home that Saturday morning, I found my nightgown solidly glued to my back. I had no way of knowing that maggots had begun to hatch in my wounds, but the incessant, itching and burning pain alerted me that something horrifically unusual was taking place beyond my view.

After tiptoeing in to check on Papa, and before an older female cousin who relieved The Woman on most weekends had awakened, I drew and heated water to help loosen the gown from my back. After the water had heated, from sheer desperation and hopes of relieving the itch, I put several overflowing capfuls of bleach into the small basin with the water.

I had heard a car drive past the house a few moments earlier and since it did not seem to stop and because I did not hear a car door close, I paid no further attention. Taking a small towel, I soaked it in the bleached water and allowed it to run down my back. Contrary to the burning sensation I had expected, the water loosened my gown and provided a soothing, drawing affect. Because the itchiness having been somewhat abated by the bleach, I was in the midst of allowing myself a deep relief-filled breath when I was startled by a movement behind me!

My sister had driven to the farm apparently not expecting to see me. She had parked her car just passed our driveway which had kept me from hearing the closing of the car door. She caught me unaware just as I was stepping out of the blood, pus, and bleached stained clothing when she walked into the back bedroom. My back was to her as she entered, and I did not have enough time to turn away. I looked at her face and saw the horror in her eyes that her mouth soon revealed. She screamed and asked if I had fallen out of a tree. My back was angry and bruised although I did not know how much. My too slow response and the look on my face must have revealed to her that I had not fallen and that I was too afraid to tell her the truth. It was then that Papa called to her, I suspected, to tell her what was actually going on, as best he knew.

Although The Woman had been careful since the first night of her stay not to inflict any torture on me within Papa's hearing, I knew intuitively, that he knew I was still in peril.

I was both grateful and disappointed when Papa called out to my sister. Disappointed because I had wanted to ask about the baby she was going to have. I was excited at the prospect of having a baby on whom to dote.

I was grateful because it allowed me time to get dressed and cover up what really must have been a horrible view of my back. It was only after I had completed dressing, as I was readying to empty the basin and rinse my gown in clean water that I saw white wiggling creatures crawling on and about my gown!

So much had happened in those past few months, I was incapable of working up any level of disgust at the sight. I simply shook my head, gathered the infested gown, washed it, and hung it to dry.

Fortunately, in my desperation to find a means in which to stop the ceaseless itching, my snap decision to use bleach, was the best uninformed decision I could have made. The drawing sensation I had felt was the effect of the bleach clearing and killing the maggots in my wounds and hastened me toward healing.

Several days later, on a Tuesday, Chinee came walking up the road toward the house. He had not been there to my knowledge since the day everyone had left the farm the day after the funeral. I was so elated that even now, remembering that moment make the hairs of my arms stand on edge. I ran to him and wrapped my legs around his waist as I jumped into his arms. Heaven could have sent no sweeter angel than my brother. I felt him stiffen and I lifted my face from his shoulder and looked into his. He was staring straight ahead with cold hate-filled eyes. I looked over my shoulder to follow his gaze and saw The Woman standing on the back porch looking in our direction. I knew I would be in for it now, but it did not matter as I would have gladly walked through fire for this wonderful moment. Whatever came next would be worth the price because I had missed my brother sorely. Besides, I hardly felt the beatings anymore and since I no longer cried out or flinched, she was finding less obvious pleasure in the beatings. They had not stopped; however, they had become less frequent.

Chinee lowered me to the ground and while she looked on, he turned me away from him, toward her, and lifted my dress to reveal my back. He took me by the hand and led me away from her view. As we walked away, Chinee yelled over his shoulder, "One more time, old woman, hit her one more time and dogs won't be able to pick up what's left of your scent!" I looked back in time to see the back door slowly closing. Chinee promised me that he would make sure that I was safe, and he would do it soon. I told him that I was ok and that I just wanted to know how he was doing and where he had been. I gleefully and silently took his promise to mean that we would be living together again soon.

As we visited, sitting on the front porch of Mother's cottage, he told me that he had been forbidden to come back home since he had been vocal in his disagreement with the arrangements our uncles and sisters had made and because he had demanded everything be returned that The Woman had stolen from mother. He told me that it was his job to worry about me and not the other way around. He left me that evening promising change! The next day, she exacted her revenge. Although she did not hit me, I would have much preferred she had.

Mere moments before the arrival of the school bus, she yelled at me from her perch in the kitchen, to come to the back porch. After I had reached the porch, she gathered up her girth and followed me out. I began to brace for what was surely to be another thrashing when she quietly, too quietly, told me to walk down the several step from the porch into the back yard. Too late, I realized her intentions. Just seconds after my feet touched earth, I looked up at her and was met full force with the contents of her chamber pot! Solids and liquid. She could not have devised a more devious way in which to humiliate me. We had no running water so I would have needed to draw bucketsful of water from the barrels in the front yard and heated them in order to wash myself, my hair and my clothes thoroughly and would need to do it all before the bus arrived, impossible. She threatened that if I missed the bus when it arrived, she had worse things planned for me during the day ahead. I hurriedly ran to the rain barrel and poured as much water as I could over my head and soiled dress. The smell of her waste caused me to spew my own stomach's contents. I had had just enough time to rinse the solids from my body and clothing when I heard the bus rattling up the hill toward the house. Soaking from head to toe and reeking from her waste and my vomit, I ran to my room, grabbed another dress and underwear, being careful not to let them touch any part of me and ran back out to the road just in time to board the bus. As I walked onboard, the children already on the bus placed their hands over their noses, leaned away from me as I passed, erupted in laughter, and pointed to me as they made up names to call me. I walked to the back of the bus, not bothering to turn around as I heard window after window opening in my wake, alerting me to their weak attempts to purge the odor from the bus.

When we arrived at school, I made sure not to leave the bus until it was emptied. I took shelter in the vacant girl's restroom, washed myself as best I could, put on the other clothing I'd hastily grabbed and threw everything else in the trash. I had no choice but to continue to wear my urine and feces reeking sneakers and pretended that the smell that arose with the heat of the day was not emanating from me.

Days later as I was sitting in the classroom finishing a math test, I was summoned to the Principal's office. To my great surprise and relief, my sister was standing there smiling. She told me that she had her husband's car for the day and had decided to treat me to a hamburger for lunch from the area's only hamburger joint, a short distance away. This was such a rare treat that I became giddy with the offer. The new Principal, (Professor Brailsford had died the day after Mother on the 4th of May), allowed me to leave the campus and off we went. What made that afternoon even more wonderful was seeing Chinee waiting behind the steering wheel. I gushed with happiness as the three of us drove away with me blissfully chatting about the day. I was careful not to mention the last punishment foisted upon me. We got the hamburgers to go but I was the only one eating or talking. It occurred to me that neither my sister nor Chinee had said a word to me since I had entered the car. I asked what was wrong, but they just smiled indulgently and rather nervously, I thought. After what seemed an hour of indiscriminate driving, I reminded Chinee that if I did not get back to school, I would be in trouble with both the Principal and The Woman once I returned home. Chinee looked at me through the rear-view mirror and said, "not anymore, Fae, never again."

I never went back to that school or to that woman. I had been kidnapped, rather that is what she and my uncles told the Sheriff when I failed to return to school after lunch. My sister and Chinee had driven for hours meanderingly up and down back roads and little traveled highways, killing time, and trying desperately not to be seen by anyone who might be persuaded to tell of our location. During that drive, they haltingly told me some of their plans and I was naturally having difficulty assimilating all of it.

We eventually doubled back briefly to my sister's In-law's home and there, by happenstance alone, my eldest Uncle reached us by telephone. He demanded that I be put on the telephone and once there, he berated me by telling me how I was killing his father! He accused me of cutting into Papa's heart just mere months after he had lost his only daughter! He asked me how I dared to hurt Papa especially since I knew that he favored me above all his grandchildren. He angrily told that he was on his way to bring me back home, over dead bodies if he needed to. I knew his threats were not idle. I heard Papa yelling in the background at my uncle, his son, telling Uncle that his would be the only dead body if he did not give him the telephone.

When Papa was on the line, I could barely hear him as my sobs had grown loud and bordered on hysteria. To be accused of doing anything to hurt Papa, hurt me more than all the months of pain and humiliation I had suffered. How could anyone accuse me of such an awful thing? None of this had been my idea and I was ready to go home simply to prove my uncle wrong! I heard Papa's voice finally break through and he was telling me to run! He was telling me to not come back to the farm because my life depended on it! She will not stop until she kills you, don't come back here Baby, this is the only way I can help you! He said further to me, "you've never disobeyed me, don't start now." I knew it was senseless to say anything other than, "Yes Papa," because he clearly would not have heard a longer sentence due to his loss of hearing and because I could not have possibly choked out a longer sentence. The last thing I had heard him say was, "Don't stop running until you're safe, I love you Sister!" Sister was what he called my Mother. It was not a slip of the tongue that he called me by his love name for her. In his way, he was telling me that he had not been able to save Mother, he was therefore saving me. As the phone was being taken from him, I pressed the receiver harder against my ear trying to hold onto the connection for as long as I could. It would be over a year before I would hear his voice again.

As I held the receiver for just a heartbeat or two longer, I heard Papa tell my Uncle, "go after her and you will never come back here and continue to draw breath."

To hear my Papa defending me against his son was overwhelming. Someone had taken the phone from me and invisible hands were suddenly and hurriedly pushing me outside toward the car. My sister had borrowed, permanently, a dress from her sister-in-law, who was similar in size to me and put it in a brown paper sack. It was all I had in the world beyond the clothes on my back and the .32 cents, the change from the hamburgers we had bought a decade ago, and which had been tied in the corner of a handkerchief and pressed into my hand.

Once again driving on backroads, Chinee and my sister drove the sixty or so miles to Beaumont and purchased one, one-way train ticket to Los Angeles. When Chinee finally finished telling me all of what was to become of me, I cried inconsolably. I clung to him and begged him to allow me to remain with him. I tried everything in every way I could to tell him I did not want to be anywhere that he was not. I told him that I was sorry for making The Woman beat me and that I would try harder not to make her angry again. "Please Chinee, don't send me away from you!" I begged. I was deep in the midst of my histrionics and therefore had not noticed the small crowd which had gathered around us, some in the crowd demanded to know if all was well.

I had screamed and begged, kicked and pleaded, all to no avail. I was being sent away, disposed of, by Chinee, of all people! Dejected, I sat down on that train platform, clinging to the brown paper sack, and prayed to die. I looked up into Chinee's eyes expecting to see firm determination but instead I saw only abject misery. I saw a heart breaking; a broken heart whose unsteady heartbeat matched that of my own. With stunning clarity, it suddenly occurred to me that every important moment in my life began and ended in those eyes and yet I had just accused him of sending me away when in actuality, the only thing he was doing was saving me, saving me yet again and for that, he would suffer.

Ever my protector, Chinee walked up and down that platform accessing each person holding a ticket. I watched him as he approached a late 60'ish lady and spoke to her while pointing toward me. She smiled, nodded, and reassuringly patted his left arm. He turned from her and returned to me. "Fae, that lady over there is going to look after you while you're on the train; she's going almost all the way to Los Angeles, so if you need anything she'll help, ok"? "Can she help me stay here Chinee," I thought to myself. I did not want to see the pain in his eyes anymore, so I just simply looked down at the platform floor and nodded.

As the conductor gave the final boarding call, I had one brief moment of panic and clung to Chinee yet again. He held me so tightly and for the first time since mother died, Chinee cried. He was losing both Mother and me, her mini-mirror image and I was losing my counterbalance in life. I did not know how to live in a world without Chinee. I did not want to know how to do so.

Quite a number of years passed before I discovered that Chinee had been arrested and placed in jail for his part in "kidnapping" me. He did not plead his case nor ask for forgiveness. He had stood steadfast in his determination that as my only brother, it was his responsibility to care for me and needed no one's permission to do so. In the face of his resoluteness and sound argument, the High Sheriff Humphrey eventually released him, to the objections of both The Woman and my uncles who had wanted to teach him a lesson in obedience and obstinacy.

Now, for the first time in my life I was to breathe air that was not scented by my brother; surrounded by light that had not touched him first. I was to walk on ground that his footsteps had not yet broken and therefore I had no trail to follow. I had always known that in Chinee, my safety rested but I had no idea or ever thought that my being safe would be coupled with leaving the only safety I had ever known. That locomotive and over eighteen hundred miles of train tracks took me further and further away from Chinee but at the same time, it took me back to him. Back to learning football, back to his last dime, back to our Spring, to Faith and Mrs. Brown and the first limo ride of my short life. That train took my mind back to days which I refused to let pass from my remembrance no matter how far I traveled. My memories of Chinee are as plentiful as there are particles of dust. They are more brilliant than the many shades of greens after a spring rain. The physical scars The Woman created upon my arms and back would fade in time and the severity of the pain would lessen with the years. But the deep emotional scars she created by causing my separation from Chinee makes my breath catch to this very day and it frustrates my attempts of total forgiveness.

May God rest her tortured soul for she very clearly had so little peace while she lived. Her daughter, the very same one who had pinched me so unmercifully during Mother's funeral, told me years later that doing lucid moments, from her nursing home hospital bed, her mother would ask of me. She also told me of the terror-filled screams which erupted unbidden from her mother night after night, unnerving other patients and driving the overnight nurses to distraction, until exhaustion and a pill or two, would finally offer her sleep. She wondered aloud to me what things in her mother's life haunted her even when the lights were on. I did not bother to offer an opinion.

Each clickety clack of the train's progress along that metal track took me in two decidedly different directions, one, took me physically further away from Chinee than I had ever been and the other took me emotionally closer to him than I could have ever hoped. Physically, there would be no more day-to-day interaction with him, no more spur of the moment memories to make, no more seeing the light of his smile before I saw his face. Emotionally closer to him because I had to be closer. As I sat in that seat next to the lady who had promised Chinee to watch over me, I made yet another vow; I was determined never to forget. I promised myself to cultivate my memories just as carefully as a horticulturist cares for his plants; to nurture my memories as a mother nurtures her child.

There is nothing as valuable as that which is sacrificed with no expectations of receiving value in return. That is true love and was certainly too mature a lesson for my tender age but an extremely appropriate one. I pressed my cheek against the train car's window and strained for a last glimpse of Chinee. That last look created the only memory I wish I could erase. He was kneeling alone on the platform, arms wrapped around himself, weeping. I fell asleep, sitting upright that first night of three, remembering his tears on my cheek and wondering and worrying...Worrying and wondering...Did I show you that I loved you enough for you to know that I did?

As I write the final words of this chapter Chinee, I have assumed the same position you were in as I caught the last glimpse of you on that fateful day...

...I L O V E Y O U C H I N E E from Earth to Heaven and every star in between, let my love of you bounce throughout the universe, gathering the light you left behind and leaving enlightened trails for me yet to follow.

In the next chapter, you will meet one of the loveliest of God's creatures, who in just three days, almost singlehandedly cancelled out "My summer of abuse". She was indeed special and deserves her very own chapter apart from Chinee. She is the reason that I stand firm in my resolve that God always places the right person in your life at the right moment.

I pray that I never forget from where my help actually comes and further pray that I never fail to give Him the Glory. Proverbs Chapter 3 verses 5 and 6 continues to sustain me.

My Brother Was My Keeper...

The Train, My Rahab, and Me

They Were Not All Bad

For a few short years, gratefully so, I had been cocooned by an extraordinary love given by extraordinary people who had known extraordinarily little love themselves. The circumstances of my life of which I have selectively shared thus far, had for a time, convinced me that I had been ill-prepared to face what was to befall me. Whereas I believed that it was simply normalcy to be nurtured by warmth and security, I learned that within my orbit, in that time and space, there were far fewer of those willing to give love freely than there were those who willingly and selfishly took from others merely because they could.

Those who give love and expect nothing except the pure pleasure there is in giving are outnumbered by those who have never given a thought to another being whereby they did not balance what they themselves would receive from such an engagement first. I despise the latter.

Although I've been burned by the unwarranted hatred of others, I have not been consumed by it and that fact has ABSOLUTELY NOTHING to do with me or anything that I have done. It does have EVERYTHING to do with the belief, faith, and hope that was planted in me, prayed over me, taught to me, and shown to me by those who were sent to prepare me and the God who delivered me and the Christ who saved me.

One of my proven mantras is, "God always sends the right person into your life at the right time." I challenge each of you to look back at some of the most difficult moments of your life and remember the person or persons who were there to help you through the process. I sincerely declare they were there by Divine Providence and not by ordinary coincidence. To this point and because I am still recovering from recalling the last chapter, I would like to focus for a moment on some of those people God placed in my path. Some were bandages for my sore spirit. Some were the laughter that I thought I had lost. Some were a soft spot to fall on a hard day. All were Heaven's Emissaries.

My dear little friend Faith and her further influences will be covered more in a later chapter. I have written rather precisely of the major affect Mrs. C. had upon me but there were others, such wonderfully, undeniably selfless others. Others of whom I would utterly dishonor had I allowed the seeds of hate spread at my feet to overtake the love vines planted by the likes of Sammie, a young man 4 to 5 years my senior who took the time to soothe the aching heart of a little girl when adults could not be bothered to do so. Sammie showed me the true size of a mustard seed and what a gigantic plant it could grow into when watered by faith. I am not surprised at all that 25 to 30 years later he followed his heart into ministry. Mrs. J. Hubbard taught me that food shared in love will fill an empty heart to overflowing. Mrs. Arleeza M. sang with such beautiful, heavenly regard that even sadness would dress itself in melancholy loveliness and tip an overturned heart upright. There might be someone reading this that will remember and perhaps invoke an altogether different or maybe similar recollection and there lies the beauty in looking back. I cherish each of these names and others.

But the name of the person of my next shared memory was never given to me but she was without a doubt the most selfless, the most giving, the most laughter spreading, contagiously charitable soul ever placed in my path and for her, I will always be grateful. One chapter will not do her justice, so please allow me to use this time simply as an introduction to a most wonderful, sadly used, terrifically abused, rescuer of one such as herself, fully discarded by all except God and me. There was a time when I truly wished she had told me her name because had she bestowed that honor upon me, I would have honored her by giving my first child her name in some form. But, by not knowing her name I am thereby forced to recognize the spirit she shared unselfishly with me and I in turn, desire ever to be that Spirit others see in me. My Papa, instructing me in being careful of the impression I left with others, told me that my name would go places that I never would. In this young lady's case, her spirit will touch unlimited souls in lands her feet never touched. I'm thrilled for the opportunity to share her loving-kindness with you.

After the Sunset Limited pulled away from Beaumont's Laurel Street station and made its first stop some 90 miles Southwest in Houston, it once again gathered its full head of steam and pressed forward toward Los Angeles. There was nothing to see outside except the darkness surrounding the train. The occasional blinking of the overhead, amber-colored lights inside the car created ghostly, elongated shadows of the seated passengers, all of which I preferred not to see.

There was exactly nothing to break the gloom that rode in that car with me except the hauntingly beautiful sound of a song that appeared to be playing repeatedly from some other car on the train. Every time the person I came to know as the Porter would enter and leave the car in which I rode, the sound of the music would be louder and clearer. I wanted to follow him and find the source of the music, but fear and insecurities kept me seated. I began trying to make sense of the few words I was able to string together. "Got to take my baby, wherever I'm bound... ease the pain...So, Mr. Conductor..."

After someone came into the car from somewhere behind me there was suddenly such a loud chorus of voices demanding in unison to: Back this train up, that it startled me and brought to mind train robberies on Westerns I had watched with Papa! It was many hours later after I had heard the same chorus of voices making the same demand when I finally understood that the voices were joining in on the refrain of a new song by new singing artist Al Green! It was October 1967 and **Back Up Train** was the latest hit song. There could have been no more appropriate song for my first lonely train ride! What's more, this particular train was occupied by car after car of military troops being shipped West and then to parts unknown and all wanting the same as me, to back the train up!

Hunger, thirst, fear, loneliness, and an increasingly difficult to suppress urge to empty my bladder made sleep impossible. The Lady into whose care I had been submitted, had entered the car, exchanged seats with me, ate a piece of fried chicken from her possessively protected, twine-tied shoebox, and promptly fell asleep with her head resting upon the window, never saying a word to me. I dared not to wake her to ask where I could relieve myself. I thought it not important enough. I did vow however, that I would ask the next person to pass how one would go about relieving oneself aboard a bunch of moving metal boxes! Trouble was, and I had no way of knowing, it was already well past midnight, and no one would be passing by for several more hours.

Somehow, I had fallen fitfully asleep and awoke to Bro. Al still pleading with the Conductor and my bladder still pleading with me. Sometime during the period after I had fallen asleep, the Lady must have awakened and partook again of her precious boxed lunch because she now held a handkerchief which was wrapped around sucked cleaned bones. (I wonder if I would have noticed how totally devoid of flesh those bones were if I had not been so hungry). I had not eaten since 11:30 the previous day and I could not remember my last restroom visit! I considered briefly asking for a piece of the Lady's chicken or barring that a piece of her bread but Mother's admonition of never letting anyone know you were hungry to avoid being taken advantage of, chased that thought away. But I was not above waking her this time to ask about a restroom! Just as I was about to shake her shoulder, a lovely, slender young woman stopped next to me and bid me good morning. Startled, I tried but failed to give voice to a greeting in return.

The previous day's crying and the lack of water had left me quite hoarse! Gratefully, she did not let my croaking dissuade her from talking further. Looking at the Lady still sleeping next to me, she asked, "Is she your mother?" I shook my head vigorously. "Your grandmother?" Again, I shook my head. She covered several other feminine relationship possibilities before she finally blurted out, "Well, what the hell you doing sitting here with her?" I did not know whether to giggle or cry; giggle was my first choice, but I was too vicariously close to wetting myself to lose myself in a fit of giggles! She told me that she had seen me sleeping the night before and wanted to talk to me because she had seen me crying on the platform and wanted to know if I was alright. *She had come looking for me*! I croaked out, "restroom," and she said, "lawd gawd, you ain't peed all night?" Again, I shook my head. "Com'on, let's go," she said. I followed.

She took me forward to the front of the car and then out. There was about a four by four foot, windowed, enclosed area between the cars with a moving left to right floor, it terrified me. She told me that we would have to jump over the moving floor to the next car since neither of our legs were long enough to simply step over. She saw the uncertainty in my face and asked if I had ever played hopscotch, nodding this time, she said, "same thing, we just moving is all." Nothing except the humiliation of wetting myself made me take that jump and the very next car held a restroom! It had been an awfully long time since I had been so grateful for anything so basic! After relieving the pressure of my bladder, my stomach was now free to voice its opposition to being neglected. Loud, angry grumbling refused to pay attention to Mother's admonitions, and she giggled as she asked me which I had been holding longer, my hunger or my water? That time I did giggle, she had such an old-person way of speaking, but I did not want her to think I was laughing at her. I needn't have worried, she laughed with me. She told me to follow her and we car hopped to the next car and miracles upon miracles there were people, tables, and food! She asked if I had any money, still unable to speak, I pulled the handkerchief from my pocket with the quarter, nickel and 2 pennies tied into the corner. She looked at me sadly and asked if I was going all the way to California with .32 cents? I knew my meager clothing was nothing of which to brag but I had not realized until then just how poor a picture I presented. My stomach chose that second and growled all the louder. She told me to sit down and order whatever I wanted. I shook my head and she told me that she would tell me to shut up if I had actually said something but, since I could not talk, to just sit down and get ready to eat! I did and had what seemed to me, the most wonderful meal of my short life! Sausage, bacon, eggs, biscuits, jelly, potatoes, and my first taste of real, fresh-squeezed orange juice, not Tang, and I did not like it, but I drank every drop. I did not know how far away California was or if I would have another meal before we arrived. She paid for our food and I hugged her and thanked her profusely. The warm food, water and juice having softened my vocal cords somewhat, I thanked her. I wanted to talk to her, ask questions and find out things about her but the heavy meal and lack of restful sleep was making it difficult to follow my own thoughts. She took me back to my car and the still sleeping Lady, whose cold chicken now just smelled greasy instead of delicious and promise to come back and check on me. I hugged her again, curled up in my seat and joined the Lady in deep, train rocking, satisfying sleep.

True to her promise, she came back and told me to hold out my hand. I did and she pressed a twenty-dollar bill into it. It took me a moment to grasp that this was something she was giving to me. The last time anyone had pressed folded money into my hands was the night Mother died (*what had happened to that money? I wondered*). She reached down and closed my fingers around the bill and told me she would see me later at supper time. She had work to do. I nodded and watched her leave. I fell asleep again in the early afternoon light thinking of her, how old she was, how pretty she was, and if she might be a waitress in the dining car. I could not wait to share another meal with her, not for the sake of eating but for the pure pleasure of listening to her speak.

My beautiful new friend was true to her word. Never did a four-hour span of time pass that she did not come to check on me, accompany me to restroom breaks, or purchase my meals. It bothered me that I had no way of repaying her.

During one of our leisurely meals, she became less reticent in her questions as to how I came to be on such a long train ride alone. The first couple of times she had broached the subject she had abruptly switched topics when tears begin to fill my eyes. But I felt I owed her something and I trusted her unlike I had trusted anyone beyond Chinee and Papa. The very least I could do was to share some of my story, besides, it had also been a long time since anyone was interested in anything I had to say. It seemed we sat hour after hour, with her asking questions and me answering and finally, me asking for her opinions to questions I had been longing to ask for months. She did not have the answers I sought but it was a relief just to be able to share my thoughts with someone so solicitous.

To assume that I did not have my own curiosity as to how she had come to be aboard the train alone would be a misguided notion, but when I asked her, I noticed a subtle but definite change in her posture, a stiffening, almost defensive. I also noticed how her right hand switched to a clenched position from a relaxed position on the table. I understood defensive postures all too well therefore, I avoided asking her anything personal again, even her name.

She could not have been more than three to five years older than me, yet she seemed so mature, so aware, and so very self-sufficient. She walked with her head held high in total defiance. I decided that I wanted to be like her, independent and immune to judgmental examinations. She received plenty of those each time we entered the dining car, at least I believed the glances were meant for her. I assumed the women who leaned slightly away from her as we walked the aisle, did so because they were jealous of the looks their male companions gave her as we passed. I had become very astute in reading body language and assessing precarious situations. We or she or I were constantly being observed and not in a kindly, caring way. My new friend paid no attention to the women or the men nor did she seem to pay much attention to just how beautiful she was. The cinnamon chocolate color of her skin combined with her soft dark wavy hair suggested strongly of a French, Spanish, and African bloodline, Creole, I decided. She had the softest Southern accent further suggesting that neither French, Spanish, nor an amalgam of either was her native language.

Early one afternoon, after my friend had escorted me back to the Sleeping Lady, boredom got the absolute best of me and I decided to display a little bravery and explore some of the cars alone. Thus far, I had been no further than the dining car, two cars ahead of us. I knew that we were near the back of the train because of the vantage point I had as we stood on the platform before boarding the train in Beaumont. Although desegregation was slowly creeping across the South, it had not yet found its way on much of the available public transportation. The Sunset had at least 30 cars and we were most likely in car number 14 or 13 counting from the front. I had made several attempts to count the cars ahead of us as we rounded steep curves to the left but never reached the same number twice. We had made several stops along the way, but I never left the train, I was much too afraid of being left behind or boarding the wrong car or much worse the wrong train!

There was not much of anything to see as I progressed forward beyond the dining car, just more of the same. People sitting, people sleeping, and every now and then a baby either crying or giggling. As I was about to enter the next car, a Porter I recognized, came through the same door toward me. He stood there and blocked my path but not in a threatening manner. *"You're a little ways away from home aren't you young lady?"* I nodded and said, "Yes," I got on in Beaumont." He smiled indulgently and said, *"Yes Ma'am, I remember where you got on, but I meant you're a long way from your car. You're not allowed to go any further forward from here."* I glanced back over my shoulder and realized that the car in which we stood was indeed just like all the others I had walked through but then realized for those few seconds as I stood there assessing the situation that the difference was that the people in this car, although Negroes, as we were called in the late '60's, wore a different style of dress. The kind of clothing that spoke of the better department stores and of dry-cleaned laundry and they wore shoes with taps on the soles to prevent excessive wear. They were those of whom I supposed, would have been called, "well-off." They had purchased tickets that did not allow them to share seats with the Whites, however, their fare did afford separation from the working-class Negroes who wore their second-hand, Sunday-best; having laundered the clothes themselves with Oxydol and blue Faultless laundry starch. This was my first-time having exposure to true classism within a race. I needed to think about this. I turned back to the Porter, thanked him, and said goodbye. *"I'll be seeing you Ma'am,"* he said showing me no less respect than if my own ticket allowed me passage in this car.

Since my trip forward had ended abruptly and because I was not quite ready to just sit and watch the scenery, I thought I would backtrack and see what the cars behind mine offered. As I walked through the car which held my seat, I glanced over at the Sleeping Lady and she was wide awake! This was a first! She looked up at me and did not seem to recognize me at all! I returned the favor! I walked through the first car and it held people who must have paid the same fare as the people in my car. There were maybe four or five men in Army uniforms. The car after that held as much cigarette smoke as it held soldiers and so did the car after that and the one after that and the next and the next! There was another dining car not quite as nice as the one I had been visiting but the food smelled every bit as good and that was where I spotted my friend. She was smiling and talking to a couple of soldiers and I was not sure if I should interrupt them to say hello. I had just decided to make a hasty retreat when she spotted me and asked if I needed anything. I shook my head and told her that I just wanted to see what else was on the train. She told me she would be by later to have dinner with me.

At dinner that evening, she seemed very pensive and not her normal talkative self. At every other meal, she had told me stories of different passengers, where they were going, their children, what type of work they did, and when they planned or if they had planned to return to wherever they had come. I did not ask how she knew; I was simply happy to be part of her conspiratorial gossip because merely from the way she had told me the stories, I could tell she had not been informed of these things by the women who leaned away from her unintentional touch. Today though, instead of eating with her normal abandonment, she simply pulled the crust from her sandwich and picked at the filling inside. Each time we had been together, she would take my hand and slide folded bills into my hands. This time was no exception. Each time, I objected, but she would not listen to my protestations. At last count, my little handkerchief, tucked safely in my front pocket, held over one hundred dollars and the corners had become harder to pull and tie together! I ate quietly, wishing I knew how I could get her to talk to me and wondered what was making her so sad. As I was finishing my last bite of burger she said, "I swear I have never seen a person who loves hamburgers as much as you do."

"I guess they remind me of the last time I had lunch with my brother," I answered sheepishly.

She reached over and handed me what felt like three or four bills. I asked her why she was doing this, but she asked me a question instead of answering mine. She asked, *"how well you know these sisters you gonna be staying with?"* I told her that my eldest sister was pretty like her, and that I had been named after her. I told her that I knew my eldest sister best because she would come home several times a year and even though she was sixteen years older than me, she did not act like other grownups, she was fun.

"Humph, People are always fun when they on vacation but get them on their regular day and they can be just as sour as everybody else," she retorted. *"What about your other sister?"*

"I don't know much about her. I think I've only seen her three times. She got married really, really young, about my age and moved away. She hardly ever came back home. When she did come home, she acted as old as my Mother and treated me like I was one of her children instead of her sister," I answered.

"*I sure am hoping you won't have to stay with her,*" she said somewhat sad, and I wanted to ask her why she felt that way but was not really certain I wanted to know the answer.

She grew quiet again and said to me, "*Look, you gotta really listen to me now ok?*" I nodded, suddenly unsure and afraid of what she was about to say. "*You had a Mama and other family that loved you, so you got that to build on. Don't let them other people who hurt you make you forget about the ones that loved you cause if you do that, you gonna let them and you down. There might come times in your life that might make you do some stuff that you don't want to do but if it means the difference between living and dying then you do it but don't live in it but most 'specially **don't let it live in you**, you hear me, Cher?*"

I blinked hard trying not to cry. I did not let any tears fall, but dang they stung me in protest to being held onto too tightly. "*We gonna be pulling into San Bernardino tomorrow and that's where I get off, that's where the lady you been sitting with is getting off too.*" I wondered how she knew that since the Lady had not spoken to me since our first night aboard and to my knowledge had never spoken to my friend either. Then it struck me afresh what she'd just said. She would be leaving the train! Fear flooded me!

"Where is San Bernardino?" I asked my voice shaking. She squeezed my hand and told me it was about 60 miles or so from Los Angeles and it would probably take about two hours to get to the station there. I did not want her to leave. I wanted to go with her, and I said as much. She told me that she had no family to go home to so she pretty much rode the trains and would get off in whatever town suited her and moved on when she got bored. I asked her why she could not stay onboard to Los Angeles since no one was waiting for her, but she said someone *was* waiting, they just weren't family. It was strange how in just three days I had become so dependent upon her and so happy to be in her company. I also felt guilty for thinking she was supporting herself by pickpocketing. So, what if she did? She did not do it just for the sake of stealing. She had no one to take care of her either and besides that, she'd given me most of what she'd taken. I promised her I would always remember her. She told me not to bother remembering her, but to remember what she had told me. We ended the meal that evening with her telling me to never expect anyone to take care of me. That it did not matter if I was only thirteen, there was work I could do and be paid a clean, honest wage for it. She told me to always keep train or bus fare home and to never, ever depend on anybody for nothing. She had said, "**Work for yourself even if you're working for somebody**!" (That took some pondering). "Don't forget that," she warned. She told me she was going to say goodbye to me now because we would be pulling into San Bernardino early and she would not have time to say goodbye. We hugged each other and she did something that I will forever believe to be the most tender, intimate, non-sexual touch humans can share with one another. She took her hand and softly caressed my cheeks first with her palm then with the back of her hand; much the same way my mother always did just before she would say goodnight to me. I did not cry...I was done crying, but my broken heart found altogether new ways and places in which to break.

I sat alone that next morning. It seemed most of the people in my car disembarked in San Bernardino. I, perhaps understandably, developed a dislike for San Bernardino and from then until now, I have never changed my opinion of that city. I did not want to sit in that seat alone, so I walked to the dining car and ordered coffee! Coffee!!! She had drunk coffee, so I would. While seated there I heard a woman sitting behind me tell another that she finally felt free to leave her husband's side for a while since the little "*la putain*" had left the train. I had absolutely no idea as to what she was referring and did not care. I was once again facing an uncertain tomorrow. As I sat there sipping my overly sweet and heavily creamed coffee, I counted the money that was now barely contained inside my now dingy handkerchief. Inside there was three-hundred dollars and 32 cents! Boy, pickpocketing could sure be lucrative if done correctly, I supposed. Maybe that was what she had meant by doing something bad to live but not to keep doing it once you got on your feet. As the train pulled into Union Station in Los Angeles...somewhere in one of the cars behind me, someone once again began to play the song, Back up Train. *How I wished it would.*

I kept my promise to my friend albeit not quite as I would have preferred. Within two months of arriving in Los Angeles I was told by my eldest sister that I would be living with my second eldest sister and man oh man my train friend had been correct. It was not ideal to say the least. I could factually say that I had fallen from the frying pan into the fire. But this story is not about my sister, only in as much as I need to tell you that she insisted I would have to earn my keep. She had secured a babysitting job for me with a neighbor, watching her three children on Friday, Saturday, and Sunday nights and she had applied for both a social security card and a job in my name at a local doughnut shop, about three quarters of a mile from her home. I was warned not to reveal my true age to the owner of the shop and that I would have to walk to get to this job that offered me split shift hours from 3 am to 7:30 am and after school from 4pm to 8pm, Monday through Thursday. Second eldest sister further warned that I was not to let my schoolwork, or the upkeep of her home suffer because of my jobs. I suppose this would be a good time to mention that her home, including me was a a household of six, she was also expecting a new baby in the Spring. My duties toward the upkeep of her home included cooking, preparing her children's school lunches, and doing laundry. There was no automatic washing machine in this "modern" California home, just a wringer washer and a clothesline out back onto which I hung eight loads of laundry per week in the good old California sunshine to dry. I was also to mop uncarpeted rooms, change bed linen on 4 beds twice a week, which made me grateful that I slept on a sofa, wash dishes twice a day and in my spare time, iron the freshly washed clothing for her family. I was profoundly grateful that I did not own many articles of clothing to add to my laundry duties. I was also to do anything else that would prevent me from sitting down for more than ten minutes and a page of schoolwork at a time. How had my beautiful train friend known what was ahead for me with this second eldest sister? I worked and I saved every dime I could after paying second eldest for my food and board, beyond what the State of California and social security paid her for offering shelter to her orphaned under-age sister.

Regardless of the situation in which I found myself in this strange, new place, I still held to the fact that God had never left my side and continued to put people into my life who had direct, positive impact upon my life choices.

The doughnut shop owner took me under her wing, taught me her business, and gave me my first detailed lessons in book-keeping and accounting, in which I would eventually work professionally and retire from after more than 50 years. Also, during that time at the doughnut shop, I found myself working side by side with a very lovely young woman of French dissent. She had been working her way across the country and so far had made it from Boston to Southern California by taking odd jobs to earn enough money to finally settle in San Francisco.

"Coast to Coast is what I desire most," was her often spoken phrase. She taught me a few rudimentary French phrases and we giggled a lot between serving up pastries and hundreds of cups of coffee per day. She reminded me of my dear Train Friend but best of all she made me forget how truly exhausted I was.

One morning, after she had completed a sale to a particularly prickly and difficult customer, she had walked away from the counter calling the woman a "*la putain*" under her breath! I asked her the meaning of the phrase and she said the politest description would be a prostitute or whore and she referred to the New Orleans sex workers. My breath caught in my throat as I remembered the women behind me in the dining car on my last morning on the train. They had been speaking about my young friend. She had once told me that she normally went as far East as New Orleans, her home, and as far West as San Bernardino stopping anywhere along the way and in between. She was not a pickpocket after all! She made her living working military transport trains! I wasted no pity on her because she needed none, nor did I change my extremely high opinion of her. She earned a living the best way she knew, hurting only herself and by doing so helped me, a lost and lonely young girl. She was my very own *Rahab*. Not for the first time, God used a prostitute to deliver one of His own and I will forever hold my train friend and the 2nd and 6th Biblical chapters of Joshua close to my heart. Despite her telling me not to bother remembering her, I've never forgotten her and never will.

My Lord, my Savior, and My Jehovah Jireh, please be attendant to the fervency of this, my prayer. Lord, whether my train friend of whom you so lovingly placed in my life is still occupying space on this side of your glory or whether she has entered into your eternal presence, I thank you for the love and wisdom you showed to me by placing her and others in my life during the times I needed them most. I thank you Lord for all your blessings and for what some would call trials. Nothing you have allowed in my life has broken me because you have been my rod and strength. Lord, if possible, I ask that you allow your obedient servants of times long ago, of whom will be known to me as my Train Friend and as Nurse Nice, until I meet them again in Paradise, to know that I've never forgotten their benevolence to me and their obedience to you. And Lord please, peer into my heart and see that I have always acknowledged Your presence in their lives and mine. It is in Your matchless name that I declare my humble gratefulness, Amen.

MY BROTHER WAS MY KEEPER...

My Wedding, Chinee, and Me

Our first argument

I t was my senior year in high school, and I had only seen Chinee once in those four years and then it was on the occasion of Papa's funeral three years earlier. It seemed we had gone our separate ways and yet there was still a calming closeness not nurtured by contact. It was during those years when Chinee had become more of an absentee guardian. He kept abreast of my comings and goings through telephone conversation with our older sisters.

During the summer just before my senior year, I met a young man and we fell in love. Our original plan was to remain engaged until after my graduation, the following June at which time we would carry out our commitment to each other through wedding vows. As fate, or more accurately second eldest would have it, our plans were ramped up significantly. On September 4th, a Saturday, as we sat around enjoying a pre-Labor Day celebration, our wedding date took center stage during the conversation. In the space of less than ten minutes our wedding, which had previously been scheduled for June of the next year, was inexplicably and resolutely changed to the upcoming Friday. This was something in which neither my fiancé nor I had any input yet, neither of us were wholly against the idea, my main concern

125

being graduation. Second eldest had found the perfect opportunity to take control of a situation and thereby became herself, the center of attention.

My desire to graduate high school before becoming married was a major irritation to her and was not something that would be allowed or discussed.

I should say here and now that my graduation would have made me the first and only of Mother's five children to graduate high school. Mother determined desire to have at least one of her children "walk across the stage" increased with each drop-out. With my being the last in school, I was just as determined to make her wish, the only thing she'd ever asked of me and the only thing that I could give her; posthumously of course. Although I had no qualms about marrying my fiancé earlier, much earlier, than planned, I wanted only to carry my maiden name and maiden experiences across that stage with me. This was not something that had any value at all to second eldest it would seem.

So, with barely a glance in our directions, second eldest boarded a train of her creation and went full steam ahead into planning my wedding with just 6 days to spare. The only request that I was granted was to call Chinee and ask that he get to Los Angeles quickly so that he could escort me down the aisle and symbolically give me away that following Friday, the 10 th of September. I had no idea the storm my request would create.

Dialing Chinee's number filled me with a celebratory exaltation. These feeling were a measure of my impending marriage but more to the expectation of seeing Chinee again and having him walk me down the aisle. I could barely contain myself while waiting to hear his voice come across the line. "Hey Chinee, I need you to get a plane ticket for next Thursday. I'm getting married on Friday and you have to be here to give me away!" There was an agonizing eon of silence that followed my announcement.

So much so that I thought we had lost our phone connection. "Chinee? Chinee, did you hear me? Are you still there?"

"Hell yea, I heard you," was his unexpected response to me. It was as if I had been sliced apart with a frozen saber. I had never heard such coldness in Chinee's voice especially when talking to me about me. I could not phantom what I had done in such a short time to have created this hostility. Neither was I equipped to handle it.

"What's wrong Chinee? What did I do?"

"Fae, how in hell can you ask me what's wrong with me, what the hell is wrong with you? You're seventeen goddamned years old. You've got like 9 months between being like the four of us or getting a diploma, what the hell are you thinking, Fae? Are you pregnant? Have you gone on to being like the rest of your sisters? Have you had trouble keeping your damned legs closed?" Saying that I was crushed would be an understatement to the same tune as saying the sun is warm. Before I could think of a response to his "pregnancy accusation," I was hit with another verbal assault. "Fae you know how much Mother wanted at least one of her kids to graduate and you're the only one left. Are you going to marry this bastard and let her down too?"

TOO? That was too much. It was all too much. After telling second eldest, an 8th grade drop-out, not 20 minutes ago, how much it meant to me to graduate first and now being accused of the very thing that I was against was just way more than I could take, and I snapped.

"If you knew how much it meant to Mother, then why didn't you graduate Chinee? Why wait for me?" My reply must have stunned him as much as his had me. But I could not stop. I have been doing what everyone expected of me all my life. I'd always done what I was told even when it broke my heart to do it. I did it all even when I was never asked my opinion, even when I was only an afterthought. And now, even NOW, I was being accused of being selfish. My very own wedding date was not in my control! My brain screamed for me to make sense of what was happening and my old friend Headache, made an appearance.

"Chinee, all I wanted was for you to walk me down the aisle and..."

He cut me off before I could say more, "If that bastard you're marrying wants you then you can tell him for me that he can have you. You don't need me to give you away, you've already done that ya damn self!" The phone went dead.

So, there began and ended the first argument that Chinee and I ever had. I was crushed that afternoon, that evening, and the day of my wedding. My brother-in-law walked me down the aisle, but I carried a little cutout photo of Chinee with me in my bouquet. He never knew that he did indeed walk down the aisle with me that brightly beautiful but slightly sad 10th day of September.

The distant that separated us that day lasted exactly nine months and three weeks. When I walked across my high school stage the following June with diploma in hand, the first person I saw was my brother standing shoulder to shoulder with my husband and smiling proudly.

I came to accept that Chinee's initial anger was not directed toward me or my new husband. It was only that he could never freely consent to giving me away. He had had to do that once when he put me on a train, and he did not expect or desire to do it again. I was still his little sister, still his responsibility, and still belonged to him. I still do.

MY BROTHER WAS MY KEEPER...
His Wedding, Chinee, and Me

It was late winter in 1977 when my phone rang early. Everything was always early when Chinee was involved. He was never late for anything that required his presence and having a telephone conversation with his baby sister required his presence. Therefore, at 6:15am on Saturday morning, my only sleep-in day of the week, the teeth jarring second ring of the telephone found me nearly peeling myself off the ceiling. "Helloooo"? as Moe said to Curly, "Top of the morning to you. Did I wake you up"? Chinee's voice boomed mimicking the characters in one of his favorite shows, The Three Stooges.

"Nah, darling", I said. "I was sitting here on the side of the bed really hoping the phone would ring, because after all it's been at least 10 hours since it last rang, and I just could not sleep for worrying that the ringer might not be working".

My sarcasm notwithstanding, Chinee continued without missing a beat, "Well as long as I wasn't the one who woke you up. You might as well just sit back, relax and talk to me a while, Johnson." I remember rolling my eyes and falling back on my pillow; resigned to the fact that my plans for a leisurely, lazy, and quiet morning in bed had just gone up in smoke. I finally giggled, reached for a cigarette, and asked him what was on his mind and why he had waited so late in the day to call me.

"Well, Johnson, it's like this, I really kinda hate to mess up a good thing, all things considered, but I think I might have to get married." I was at first shocked and speechless and then this rumbling sound began in my stomach mimicking the forerunner of massive diarrhea and finally materialized in my throat in the form of a gut-busting fit of laughter and had me doubled over in the throes of hilarity. I could not believe that my brother had gotten someone "in trouble" and I was thrilled at the prospect! After I finally got my breathing under control and was once again able to carry on with the conversation, I asked him which part was going to mess up the good thing, the baby, or the marriage. It was his turn in the gut busting machine. "Nah, Johnson. It's not like that. You know you and Charles are the only two people that I know whose marriage has gray hair. Ya'll been around a few years, (it had only been about 6 years at that point). You know there hasn't been a long-lasting marriage in this family since Papa and Mama (our grandparents). But anyway, Fae, I met an ole girl and I think I might just be ready to get married.

"Great Gosh Almighty Man, have you asked her yet? What's she like? I know she's got to be at least a year or two older. You have never in your life dated anyone the same age as you. You know that I know that you have a thing for older women don't you, Allen? So, who is she?

"Ok, ok. Take a breath Johnson."

Nope you called me! Called me, brother dear, and woke me up to boot, I get to ask whatever I want to. Now start with some answers. I hope she has money!"

We both giggled and for the next hour and a half. He told me about her laughter, how old she was, where he'd met her, how much he loved her, and pondered aloud what Mother would have thought of her. All the while. I commented where I thought I should and tried to keep up with my end of the conversation, but my head was buzzing, and my heart was heavy.

I had never contemplated Chinee belonging to anyone except me. I never envisioned sharing my brother with another woman. I began to understand his reluctance in accepting my marriage. I felt so very selfish and frightened. The fact that I was losing my brother was my only thought and it broke my heart. While dog paddling in my own pool of self-pity, a quiet voice spoke to me deep inside and told me to imagine Chinee's loneliness. Mother had been gone from his life for over 10 years and still the pain of losing her was fresh. I had left him, though not by choice, at the same time and he had only allowed himself to become close to one other person during that time and that relationship had not panned out, to both their disappointment. So here now, was a chance for happiness for my brother and I would be damned before I allowed my selfishness to overshadow his joy.

I snapped out of my reverie just in time to hear him speak her name, Charlotte. I thought it was so appropriate that we had each found life partners whose names were so similar, my Charles and his Charlotte, amazing.

"Chinee," I said, "If she makes you smile so deeply that I can feel it over the telephone line and if you love her so much that it makes your heart ache to be apart from her and if her eyes light up each time she sees you watching her, then Mother would have loved her all the more for pulling that smile across your face. I've never known you to be so openly happy, Chinee, and I adore her for making you feel this way. I love her for giving that back to you. I only have two questions, Chinee, have you popped the question yet and what are you afraid of messing up?"

"Fae," he said, "We get along so well right now that I'm scared that a piece of paper might change things."

"You're right, Chinee, it will change things. It will make things better. So why haven't you asked her yet?"

"Well, Johnson, to be honest, *I'm worried about you*."

That brought tears to my eyes quicker than anything had since climbing on that train so many years ago and seeing my brother disappear on those tracks as the train pulled away.

"Why are you worried about me, Chinee? Afterall, you have always said that out of the five of us you never worried about me because you knew I would always land on my feet. I must admit that I sort of wanted you worry about me a little, just to show me you cared but eventually I understood what you meant. So, what's with the worry now?"

Well, Baby Sis, it's like this. I've already told Charlotte that as much as I love her, you would always oversee certain things in my life. That was just my way of letting her know where you fit in my life. She knows how much I love you, Fae, and I need you to know that too. Fae, I've tried your whole life to be the kind of brother to you that Mother's brothers were to her. I love you Fae, sometimes like now, the way a father would love a child, but you will always be my little sister no matter how old you get. I don't want you to think that there won't be enough room in my life for you or that I still won't be looking out for you. I need you to understand that, Fae.

"I understand Chinee," I said through streaming tears. "I love you more than you could ever know, Chinee, and please, please, please Chinee, don't ever make another important decision that will affect your life by wondering how that decision will affect me. I love you, Chinee."

"I love you, Fae, now come be my Best Man!"

"I can't do that baby boy. I have to be on that front seat watching you as mother would have and besides, how would it look to have your best man balling her eyes out and using your tie as a handkerchief?"

"You know, Johnson, I see your point, put Charles on the phone."

And so, this was how it came to be that Chinee asked my husband to stand up as his best man at his wedding although seven years earlier he had refused to stand up for me at mine. It was his way of repairing what he thought was a weak link in the chain of our life. Didn't I tell you that there was never a better brother?

MY BROTHER WAS MY KEEPER...

Cancer, Chinee, and Me

This chapter surpasses all others in difficulty. Thinking about its contents is overwhelming. Writing about it was nearly impossible and almost the undoing of this whole story. There will be very few lighthearted moments in this chapter. There will be, as hard as it is to believe, a deepening of the love we shared, a silent acknowledgment of an unbreakable bond born of love and trust and strengthened by adversity and pain. As difficult as this was to put into words, I yet feel his presence, still looking after me and encouraging me to "Write on, Sis!" To this I answer, "RIGHT ON, BROTHER!"

Chinee had so few deep desires in life and even those, life seemed to be bent on denying him. His hope of someday playing football professionally was dashed early on when after fainting one day, extensive medical tests revealed a heart problem and early onset diabetes. Some of you might remember the late defensive lineman Ernie "Fats" Holmes of the 1970's Pittsburg Steelers Steel Curtain. He and my brother played the same positions in High School in Wiergate, Texas. Many including myself thought that Chinee was a better player if only by inches, but oh, when those two ran a safety blitz it was a thing of beauty. Watching his teammate sail into the Pros was a difficult and melancholy pill to swallow. Chinee was told of the dire consequences of not taking his condition seriously. It was explained that loss of limbs, blindness, and premature death would be a direct result of not following doctors' orders. Therefore, Chinee became very vigilant at keeping his diabetes under control and nothing else troubled him if his levels tested between 75 and 150.

Needles and test kits were a daily part of his life and all other ailments were just bothersome annoyances to be ignored. Headache? No problem, glucose level is fine. Chronic cough? Not to worry, glucose is OK. Back Pain? Chill man, my sugar is under control. It was this single-mindedness approach to major problems that had driven Chinee's life. Although always a deep and thoughtful thinker, Chinee's mien was to take the simplest approach to solve a problem. Hungry? Eat! Tired? Sleep! Broken? Fix it! Can't fix? Walk away! Take care of the immediate problem and everything else will settle to the lowest spot. This determinate attitude was demonstrated again as Chinee was personally introduced to the "C" word.

Medical tests administered after a particularly difficult breathing episode, revealed the absolute necessity for what turned out to be quadruple bypass surgery. The healing process was slow but steady. Quite true to form, Chinee decided that all that was required to return to optimal health was his desire to recover and that would be that. And it was, for a while. A subsequent follow up visit revealed an unusual spot on the lower right quadrant of his right lung. It was a small spot and no reason for alarm the doctor said. No alarm? No reason to be upset? Nothing to worry about? OK! The hidden messages in these oft used medical sentiments seem to be meant by doctors to lessen the initial shock of their proclamations and thereby minimize any undue alarm; yet still gently and subliminally suggesting the patient to do the exact opposite..., be alarmed. Chinee wasn't. The message was too oblique. Chinee was a natural Defensive Linesman. Show him offensive movement and he would penetrate past the line and disrupt the advancement. On that same visit, the doctor told Chinee that his glucose levels were elevated, and he needed to get that back under control. Something to defend, YES! Unwittingly that doctor, that day, had a hand in sealing Chinee's fate. He negated the immediate need for Chinee to do something about the spot on his lung but validated the necessity for Chinee to take immediate action toward lowering his blood sugar levels. Even on the day he died, his blood sugar levels were under control.

Stage 4 lung cancer was pronounced nine years later. I was at home in California waiting to hear the diagnosis and the prognosis. Chinee's voice over the past several months had become several octaves higher and another chronic cough had been accompanied by blood-tinged spittle.

I recognized. I feared. I knew that Chinee had worked years as a truck driver delivering goods into and out of Naval Shipyards and other companies that dealt heavily in asbestos laden products. I knew, yet I waited hopefully for that phone call to come from Texas.

I was told by second eldest, who had relocated back to Texas, and my next to youngest sister that upon hearing the word "terminal," Chinee simply got up and walked out of the doctor's office without asking a question or uttering a sound. Out of the three remaining sisters, I alone knew why he had left that office without speaking. There had been a playing field, the doctor's office. There was a quarterback, the cancer. There was a great defensive player, himself. What there wasn't, was a workable blitz, a good defensive strategy that he could devise. Can't fix? Walk away. There was a quiet strength in the action he chose.

The horrendous proclamation of terminal lung cancer was the first of a one-two combination punch which would have landed a lesser person on his knees waving a white flag of surrender. But not my brother. He had taught me to stand strong and firm in the face of adversity. He could not have taught me that lesson had he not himself learned it and lived it. Just two months later, Hurricane Rita ripped through Southeast Texas coastal towns and communities with such fierce devastation that only a very few escaped unscathed. Except for several small precious possessions, Chinee lost his home and most everything contained within it. Rita served as the reminder that when you thought things could not get worse was when they usually did. Now homeless and dying, Chinee became the strongest most determined and deliberate that I had ever known him to be.

Chinee began planning right away. We were just a few weeks into the New Year, a year in which second eldest had proclaimed he would not live to see. Chinee determined that since life was not his to live then death and cancer would have to become submissive to his will. He would not let death claim him on any terms other than his own. Because of his difficulty breathing, it took weeks for him to tell me of all his personal and business attachments. He had already assigned his Power of Attorney over to me and presented the hospital with a DNR (do not resuscitate) order. Chinee had been given six to eight months to live. Initially he did not want to know of any pronounced time restraints upon his life. He and his wife had had numerous delicate, loving, and meaningful discussions. He and I talked by phone hours every day. I would fly to Texas as often as I could, but the phones were our most consistent link. Those conversations were precious to us both. He never asked for either the Morphine or Dilaudid, pain relievers, which were both readily available to him, for fear of having his mind clouded. I found out later, thanks to a dear friend, that he was afraid that the narcotics would put him to sleep and therefore he would miss my calls. Time was running out for both of us and I lost my resolve during one particularly poignant conversation. I painfully told him that I did not want to live in a world where he wasn't. Uncharacteristically, Chinee yelled at me. He told me that I would go on living and that he would continue to live through me but unlike him, I had a choice in the matter. He softened and told me that I had to live, or our love would die.

He denied me the opportunity to feel pity for myself, thankfully. He also would not let me know of the intense pain that he suffered. On one of my many trips home to visit with him, during that excruciating period, my husband accompanied me. Chinee asked me to go and buy him a soda and I was happy to do so. While I was out of his hospital room, Chinee told my husband of the intense pain he was in. The cancer had found its way into the bones of his ankles and shoulder. I cannot begin to imagine how agonizing it had to be for him to just lie in that bed, yet while I was with him, he insisted on walking himself to the bathroom and dressing himself. He was still setting an example for me to follow and in his own way he was still protecting me by not inflicting pain on me by withholding his pain from me. He would however allow me to apply lotion to his drying and cracked skin and I took pleasure in offering him even that small bit of comfort. He took my hand one day and told me that he wanted me to write his obituary because he knew I would do it differently. He said my words would make him seem real rather than a memory.

I could not imagine that he could ask anything more difficult until he told me that he also expected me to plan his funeral service; something that I had never been involved in any remote sense of the words. My resolute pledge made on the day of mother's funeral some forty plus years ago came rushing back to me and settled achingly underneath my heart. I had promised that I would never let him down in his time of need no matter what he may ask of me. My frightened twelve-year-old self peered out from eyes years older and took a special pride in the fact that a promise once made was soon to be honored and she sighed painfully.

On a Sunday night in mid-August, not even a month since my last flight home, I was making arrangements to fly out again when a strong yearning to speak to Chinee overcame all other thoughts. I had talked to Chinee just a few hours earlier and he had sounded extremely tired. I promised him that I would call before I went to bed that night. Although I was hours away from falling exhaustedly into my bed, I felt a yearning to call Chinee right away. When the phone in his hospital room was answered, the voice on the other end was unfamiliar to me. I felt that somehow some usurper had walked into that place where I should have been, and resentment rode hard through my soul. Please give my brother the phone I asked this un-named voice. My request was met with a request from "the voice" that I identify myself. All my reserve was slipping away. Just as I was about to throw out a swift retort, I heard what sounded like intensely labored breathing in the background. "Is that my brother's breathing that I hear." I demanded, "Is that Chinee"?

"Are you the sister named Fae?" the voice again questioned.

"Who are you and why aren't you answering me, put his nurse on the line now."

"I'm sorry, Fae, I'm your brother's pastor."

That only heightened my anxiety and I was very close to telling him that I did not care who in hell he was but that was when he told me to hold on and he would place the phone to Chinee's ear. (*Place the phone to his ear? Not hand him the phone?*) Alarms sounded in my ears and the room began to spin. "Not yet God", I prayed, "please not yet. I have to be there God, please don't take him without my being there God," I kept praying.

My mother's youngest brother was a fearsome though beloved presence in our lives. He was the self-appointed disciplinarian in the absence of a father-figure. Although it was never spoken of aloud, we, my four siblings and I, acquiesced this position of honor to our uncle. Life sometime appears cruel as it did with this uncle. Despite having an exceptionally large family, our uncle found himself alone at the end of his life with no love ones present at the moment of his death. This haunted Chinee for years and he felt that it must be the epitome of loneliness and aloneness to have no one by your side at the end of life. He and I had discussed this in painful detail, and I knew that Chinee somehow expected the same end for himself and I, as always, vowed that I would do all in my power to prevent it from being so. I promised to be with him in his final hours if it was God's will and he promised the same to me.

Unbeknownst to me, Chinee rallied a bit and gestured to his Pastor to place the telephone on the pillow next to his ear when he understood that it was me on the phone and so it was that I spent the next 3 hours talking to my brother as I listened to his ragged and shallow breathing. I told him how much I loved him and how much I had depended on him. I told him everything again that I had told him during the past 12 months; because Chinee had seen fit to laugh in the face of his six months prognosis and thereby doubled his odds. I told him how empty the world was going to be without his laughter and through the sounds of his hard-fought breaths and the sound of my heart breaking I heard a muffled and quiet "I love you, Fae," come through the telephone. For the next hour, I heard nothing more except long pauses in his breathing during which I alternately prayed would not continue and offered heartfelt gratitude seconds later for his next inhalation. Just as I was beginning to get hoarse from talking three straight hours, I heard Chinee call my name. He sounded so very tired and weak. He asked me if I was still there and through blinding tears and a failed attempt at strength of voice, I assured him that I would stay on the phone as long as he wanted. He again told me through chapped and dry lips that he loved me. I found the courage from someplace deep to ask him why he had fought so hard to stay here when God was so obviously calling his name.

Fourteen years have passed since the events in the previous paragraph, yet fresh tears are staining my face and my heart is studded with the all too familiar painful pricks of his loss. This pain has not lessened with time although at times I can now smile when I think of him, which needless to say, is often. It is so exceedingly difficult to believe that someone can truly be as selfless as my dear brother was on the night that he again saved me from that murky pool of darkness which purposed to engulf me. At a time when he could not save himself; when whatever conscious thoughts that he possessed should have been of him he again thought of me.

"Chinee, why didn't you answer Gods' call, Darling, why didn't you answer when He called your name?" Those questions were asked for him see my willingness to allow him to leave the realm of pain that had engulfed him. In his exhausted and spent state, he spoke words that I will always equate with true and unflinching love. I heard words of the ilk that I had longed to hear so many years before when he told me that he knew that out of the five of us I would always land on my feet. I heard words spoken to me that held no bounds to the limit of love "because I was worried about leaving you, Fae." Again, as he had that day in 1977, when he had told me of his impending engagement, he told me that his worries for me kept him from doing something for himself. Then, it was proposing to the lady of his dreams, now, it was escaping the painful grips of Cancer.

MY BROTHER WAS MY KEEPER...

The Feathers, Chinee, and Me

My perception of love had just been irrevocably altered. I had heard of people who have thrown themselves in front of a bullet to protect a loved one. I had read of soldiers, who without a moment hesitation, had thrown themselves onto grenades to save fellow soldiers. There are many documented occurrences where mothers, fathers, siblings, and friends have jumped instinctively into the depths of water to save a drowning child or friend only to be swept away themselves. These, to my mind, are examples of what love was meant to be. There is no love greater than what Jesus has shown to us, to willingly give up life in order for those whom we loved to gain life.

Chinee gave that to me during those early fresh hours of Monday, August 15th. During those hours when angels attended him, offered intercessory prayer for him, and prepared him for his heavenly journey. He prayed for me. He prayed for my strength and he prayed and asked God to watch over me. I know this because he told me.

Later that Monday afternoon after unsuccessfully trying to find a flight home, I called Chinee and told him that I still was trying to get to him. He told me to sit still. Although he was still drained from the previous night and he used fewer words to communicate with me; I knew that he was telling me not to come. "But, Chinee, we promised each other that…"

He cut me off and said, "no need."

"I'm still going to try to get to you, Chinee," I whispered to him and I heard him grunt a negative response. I told him that I could hear that he was tired, and I knew that the nurse, who was holding the phone to his ear, needed to attend to him. I promised to call him in two hours when I arrived home from work. The last words I told him were these, "Chinee, I love what you did for me last night but when God calls your name the next time, I want you to answer. Don't try to talk Chinee, just listen to me for a second or two. You have raised me and taught me more than anyone else in my life ever could have. You taught me by example and I'll never be able to show you the changes you have made in my heart, but I want to give you the assurance that although I will miss you with every fiber of my being, I don't want you to miss one day in Heaven because you're worried about me. As a matter of fact, Chinee, when you get there or when you're on your way, if you happen to think of me, just send a white feather in my direction. I could hear him give a weak laugh and as that sound reached across the miles, I strained to remember his laughter the day I ran away from his goal. I could hear his booming laughter the day he heard my youngest son speak for the first time. I so especially remember him laughing at his favorite television show, The Three Stooges and his favorite cartoon character, Leghorn Foghorn and most especially good ole Barney Fife! It did not matter how many times he had seen the same episodes; his laughter was just as fresh as it had been the first time he'd viewed it. I remembered his laughter as I envisioned my brother, the practical joker, chasing angels around heaven to get the whitest, softest feather to send to me. I whispered my love and promised to call back soon.

When I arrived home that afternoon, spent with sadness and emptiness, my husband met me in the garage. As we were walking the path toward our back door, I looked across the expanse of our backyard's lawn and it was the greenest and healthiest it had ever been. But there was something lying there which was strikingly out of the place. I anxiously looked up into my husband face as I pointed to the article lying there just steps away from us. At first and momentarily his reticence confused me until I remembered that he had no idea of the conversation Chinee and I had earlier. I walked across the lawn and bent to pick up the whitest, softest feather I had ever seen. I told my husband of my conversation with Chinee then rushed inside to phone him.

His wife answered the phone and it surprised me that she was there instead of work. Early on, she and Chinee had agreed that she would continue to work to make sure their medical coverage would remain in effect. Although she much preferred to be by Chinee's bedside, they recognized the sheer practically of her continued employment. Knowing this, her presence there puzzled me even more. "Is everything ok?" I asked her, desperation rising in my throat, the feather being crushed in my hand.

"He's ok, Fae," she said. "My Sweetheart asked me to spend the evening with him so how could I turn down such a nice date? Wait a minute, Fae. He knows you're on the phone and he is motioning for the receiver." She held the phone to Chinee's ear, and I could hear the rattle in his throat and my heart throbbed. It was not a sound I ever wanted to hear again. I wanted to encourage Chinee to rally again but then I remembered my promise to him that I would be fine. I forced more strength into my voice than I felt and told him about finding the feather. A little stronger chuckle tempered with more rattling told me that he understood and remembered the significance of the feather to me. What he uttered next would be the last time that I would hear my brother's voice.

"That's mighty fine Fae, mighty fine." Oh, how I wish I could have known this would be the last time I would hear that wonderfully comforting voice. If only I had known that I would not have another opportunity to tell him how much I loved him. It did not matter to me that I told him I loved him to the point of irritation because even so, it did not feel to me that I had told him enough.

Chinee died approximately eighteen hours later. I was sitting at my desk, on the phone discussing some paperwork concerns with his Hospice nurse, when over the hospital's loudspeaker I heard, "*CODE BLUE ROOM 307...CODE BLUE ROOM 307... STAT!*"

"That's my brother's room!" I yelled to the nurse. "Has my brother coded? *HAS HE CODED?*" I demanded.

"I'm sure you must have heard wrong, Mrs. Johnson," but I heard the apprehension in her voice and her anxiousness to get me off the phone was clear as well. "I'm going to go and check on your brother and call you back directly," she said but before I could ask her not to hang up, she did.

I will not go into the last moment of Chinee's earthly life, but it is necessary for me to say that he was not alone when he left this world. Chinee had orchestrated his final movement by having a dear and understanding Aunt with him at that moment. To this Aunt, I'm forever grateful for being where I could not because I could not persuade nor manipulate fate to act in my favor the night before by offering me a flight to my brother's side.

I continued to hit redial until someone finally answered the phone in Chinee's room and told me that the hero of my life was no longer occupying the part of the world in which I moved. I remember leaving my desk, but I don't remember the trip down the corridor nor descending the stairs which I had to negotiate to leave the building. What I do remember is arriving in the parking lot and seeing that the front of my car was almost sur-rounded with downy soft white feathers.

With tears stinging my already swollen lids, I looked heaven-ward and laughed! Deep within my heart I heard him laughing too, only so much stronger, and louder than I had ever heard him.

My Brother Was My Keeper...

Me

I was conceived of desire, born in shame, abandoned by guilt, and left motherless by death; I am an extremely careful measure of oh so simple complexities. I was abused by those who should have been trustworthy and maltreated by those who were already trusted. I am by all measure a large portion of complex simplicities. Despite all of the misguided deeds of the maladjusted miscreants in my life, I was rescued, nurtured, and reshaped by my brother and our Heavenly Father, into whose care he had finally entrusted me and because of it all, became the person I am today.

If it has not yet become apparent, I adored my brother. There is an extremely strong case here for hero worship and I would be a living example of just such a syndrome. Before continuing with this chapter there are a few items I'd like to expound on.

Just a little less than a month before Chinee died, I paid my last visit to him. It was mid-July. Hot, steamy, and thunderous storms passed over every couple of hours it seemed. I had made my way to the hospital, wanting to be there to help him with his breakfast, (the cancer had left his shoulder and other large bones extremely brittle and his diseased shoulder had made it almost impossible for him to lift eating utensils). Just as he signaled me, by nodding, that he'd had his fill, a deafening clap of thunder sounded just overhead and literally shook everything in his room. He raised his eyebrows and looked knowingly at me. I did not try to hide my fear and it was profoundly obvious that my paralyzing phobia of thunder and lightning was as present now as it had been when I was much younger.

During those dreadful early spring and summers storms, of which are common occurrences along the Gulf States, I made it my singular ambition to search for someone, anyone, wearing a shirt or apron whereby I could hide underneath it. If the storms happened at night, after bedtime, I would find the closest occupied bed and hide my face in the occupier's shoulder and upper arm.

As the lightning illuminated the darkened early morning sky and announced the arrival of the next clap of thunder, Chinee patted the mattress, and that signal was the only signal that I needed. I was on that bed with him in seconds with my face buried into his "good" shoulder. He chuckled as I pressed my face harder with each subsequent flash of lightening!

Some might scoff at my revealed weakness but to this very day, no matter where my children are, if they know that I am in the midst of a thunderstorm, they are either trying to get to where I am or failing that, they will call and remain on the phone with me until the storm passes. My husband would probably pay market prices to have a thunder producing button installed in our homes just for the times when my gentle reminders, begin to sound to him like unending nagging, because he knows that just a small clap of thunder will send me flying into his arms, silently surrendering, and permanently forgetting my gentle reminders.

During the moments that it took for the storm to pass and remain thunder free, I began to tell Chinee why Mrs. Adams was lashing me that long-ago day on the playground. He began to smile but then a scowl settled upon his face. I supposed, he was recalling that particular morning on a small country school campus far and away from where we now lived. I smiled at his stern face and kissed the top of his head where soft curls out-lined his features when just a few months earlier his hair had been the first casualty of aggressive though only palliative che-motherapy. As I tentatively left the safety of his shoulder, he returned my smile as he realized that something lay behind mine. We had never spoken about that beating or that morning. I do not even believe that Chinee ever mentioned it to Mother. As always, he saw me as his responsibility. I do believe however, that he must have had a word or two with Mrs. Adams because she would never look directly at me when our paths crossed although I do remember some rather strange sidelong scowls being sent in my direction.

Sitting now on the side of his bed, the storm having passed, I revisited the day of my "altercation" with Faith. He chuckled as he also remembered the tiny little girl who seemed to always be with me. "Fae, she was like a real live doll to you wasn't she"?

"Yea, she was," I replied thinking back. 'She made me feel as if I had a little sister." I really loved her Chinee."

"So, what ever happened to her?" Chinee asked me.

"I don't know," I told him but then went on to tell him about mine and Faith's sing song chatter which included the Chocolate Cake, the color Yellow and finally the "Brudda" comments. "Chinee," I said, "I know that I was only about 12 ounces and maybe a half inch taller than Faith, but you would have sworn that I was a Cruiser weight boxer fighting a feather weight! It was just awful!"

"And this was all because she was *about to call* me Brudda?" Chinee asked.

"No!" (Still selfish to the core and self-righteous as well, I was). "It was because she was *claiming* you as her Brother, her Brudda actually, and the manner in which she said "brother" somehow seemed more intimate and endearing." Although I would not have had the words to describe those feelings at that tender age, in my mind, her soon to be spoken announcement was a clear call to action.

I felt the bed shaking and thought that he was being attacked by another round of coughing, but I soon realized that he was at the beginning of one of his giant belly ripping laughs! We both let the moment have its way with us. So much so that as his doctor entered the room, he immediately joined in our infectious laughter, totally unaware as to why we were laughing. All seriousness returned after the doctor left the room. That's when Chinee asked me again if I knew what had happened to Faith. "I really don't know, Chinee. That part of my memory is quite muddy. It just seems to me that she disappeared one day soon after that playground incident. I seem to remember waiting for her in our spot on the playground one day and she never came." Unexpected tears stung my eyes as I felt her loss anew. "I seem to remember hearing, sometime later, that her family had moved to Hemphill or Toledo Bends are some such place," I said as much to the room as I did to Chinee. Chinee told me that her family had indeed moved to Hemphill, Texas and there had been some type of trouble within her family after the move. I sensed that he knew what the trouble was but chose not to tell me and I did not ask. What could it possibly matter now?

All too soon, the last day of my visit came and I needed to start for the airport some ninety miles away. As we began our farewells, I hugged him as hard as I dared and kissed the top of his head for what must have been the twentieth time, Chinee grabbed my hand as I turned to walk away. (*The hand thing still bothered me, especially in hospital settings*). I turned back to him expectantly. "Fae, find that girl and apologize." I smiled wistfully and told him that I had looked for her over the years and had never been successful. As if I had never spoken, Chinee repeated, "Fae, find that little girl and apologize."

I kissed his head for the twenty-first time and whispered, "I will Chinee, I promise." Thinking all along that again I had promised the impossible.

I had been back at work for a couple of weeks when just for the heck of it, I visited a particular website and keyed in Faith's given and maiden name and the last state of which I knew she had lived. Without expecting any results, I was dumbfounded when approximately 45 "Faiths" appeared in that general geographical area. Perhaps none of them would be her but there was one – only one, whose birth year matched hers and more importantly, there was only one that listed her married name joined with a hyphened middle name that I knew to be her maiden name! There it was now where it had not been before. My hands began to tremble as I began to doubt my sanity. What was I doing? Faith was a part of such a long-ago life but now sitting here looking at her name emblazoned across my 20-inch monitor, my once firm memory of her became watery, dreamlike, and just beyond my reach. Perhaps I had dreamed that whole episode? NO! It was not a dream and I had promised Chinee that I would find her. I just never thought that it would be this simple.

I whooped and called my assistant over to witness my find. "But after all this time, what if she doesn't remember you? How will you ever know whether she is the right person or not?" she asked me.

"I'll know her voice," I said, "I'll know her voice." Skepticism and some concern showed on her face I as picked up the phone and began dialing across the decades.

She did not answer but my disappointment was short lived when her away voicemail message began in her own voice! It was HER! She still had the barest hint of that same sweet speech impediment from years past. I could not believe that it could be that simple. I had found Faith! I left a message, crossed my fingers, and said a silent prayer.

She called me the next day with just a box car full of uncertainty in her voice. In my message, I had told her of our months of being bosom buddies and of her unannounced disappearance from my life and of my years of intermittent searches for her. I could hear even in her silence that something was bothering her about this whole conversation, so I stopped speaking to allow her the opportunity to speak openly and honestly to me.

That pause between ending my speech and Faith beginning hers seemed longer than our separation and it filled me with dread.

I steeled myself against my imaginings of her informing me how I had given her a lifelong complex because of the beating she had taken at my hands and that complex had forever prevented her from making lasting friendships. I was expecting her to tell me that she had been so scarred by the playground incident that she was still praying for retribution. Above all, I feared that most. But, it was all so much worse than that! I had almost wished that she would have begun cursing my very life. I would have preferred that she had asked me how dare, I think myself so important to her that I could just sidle back in her life after what I had done to her. But, instead, she just simply did not remember me! I was crestfallen, no longer self-centered but wholly & genuinely disappointed because I was expecting to connect with the person who had made my first years away from home joyously meaningful.

Faith heard the unspoken disappointment in my voice and true to her gentle nature, she sought to comfort me. I realized that I was crying at my desk and fought hard to pull myself together. Then she wondered aloud as to whether I could possibly be the little girl of an uncertain memory or perhaps dream she had in which she attended a different school than the one of which she had graduated. She told me that she could only recall that there was a little girl with whom she had always played with but could not remember the little girl's name. *I was that girl!* At that point, we both became emotional. Several traumas in her young life had served to blunt a good deal of her early recollections, just as Chinee had suggested. I promised to call her that evening and share my memories with her.

I did.

When we spoke that evening, I apologized for fighting her although she had no memory of the incident. She did giggle with delight when I told her how she had gotten up from the dirt and ran for help when Mrs. Brown began to teach me a much-needed lesson. The conversation naturally turned to Chinee and she asked me how "my brother" was doing. I told her that he was being hospitalized in Beaumont at Baptist hospital due to his terminal illness. I told her about how he had been diagnosed with Stage 4 lung Cancer just about 11 months earlier. A tiny knowing sigh escaped her lips although she tried to cover quickly, too quickly by asking how I was coping.

Those two-hour passed unbelievably quickly; both of us needing to break the connection but neither of us wanting to. She was trying so hard to flesh out a small memory and I was just grateful to have found her and know that she had not spent years hating me. As we prepared to end the call, I told her that I wanted to give her something that she should have had years ago but I was too selfish to give it to her. I gave her permission to claim Chinee as her Brudda! It was all that I had to give and all that she had wanted. We were both too emotionally spent to say much after that however, we did manage to swear to stay in touch.

A couple of days just beyond a week later I was thrilled to see Faith's mobile number appear on my telephone's caller I.D. display. With that recognizable and still familiar giggle in her voice, she dared me to guess where she had just been. Impossible as that was, I played along and unsurprisingly all three of my guesses were wrong. I just left from visiting our Brudda!

"Oh Fae, you were so right he knows so much about my family and his memory is just as strong as yours!" Saying that I was overjoyed would be so inadequate. I could not make my heartbeat slow down!

The gratefulness that I was feeling was inexpressible. My mind could not wrap itself around the fact that this dear, dear woman would take a day out of her busy schedule, drive almost a hundred miles, and spend the afternoon with my brother.

"Fae, it was too amazing! He even told me where to find some of my father's people right there in Beaumont." A universe sized grin would not leave my face and my cheeks began to ache as I listen to her describe her visit with my br... our Brudda!

"It was so quiet in his room when I first got there, and he seemed like he was tired and needed to rest," she told me. "I didn't plan on staying there awfully long. But once I introduce myself, Fae, he seemed to perk up and he had so much he wanted to talk to me about. Even though it was obvious to me that he was really tired he insisted on filling in some missing pieces in my life. I went there to meet him and to visit him for you, but he gave me so much Fae!" Her sweet voice caressing each word with gratitude.

My voice cracking with unspeakable emotion I managed to squeeze out an inadequate thank you through constricted vocal cords and said, "Yea, that's our Brudda, always so ready to give."

"Fae, it felt as if I had known him all my life. We had an instant connection."

"You have known him all your life. Faith," I said, "You just forgot that you knew."

She went on to tell me about there being several other women in his room when she arrived and how one of them made it obvious that she was not happy about Faith's impromptu visit.

I offered her physical descriptions of several people and as close as we could both determine, one of my more colorful outlines fit second eldest to a tee.

"Did she appear to be watching you rather than looking at you?" I asked her.

"Yes, now that you mention it, that is exactly what it felt like. But Fae, I was enjoying my visit so much with Chinee that I totally tuned her out."

"Faith, I'm afraid someday probably sooner than later, you'll find out exactly why she was watching you so closely. There is no threat to you but once you made it clear that you were a friend of mine, you immediately became an enemy of hers. Someday, I'll tell you all about my sister, second eldest. But I don't want to ruin the rest of your story by injecting more of her into it. Tell me more about your visit with Chinee." And she did, for the next thirty minutes she told me in excruciatingly beautiful detail of her reunion with our brother. Now, Chinee knew with certainty that I had kept my promise to him to find Faith. Since his death, it has become clear to me why it was so important to him for me to find Faith.

Chinee closed a long-opened chapter in our lives. By insisting that I find Faith, he was giving me additional gifts. Acknowledging that I would have no other close familial relationships beyond him, he knew that only Faith would be able to provide the support I would need to get through his death. She and I having a foundation and history built totally upon love, much the same as his and my relationship. He had made sure that I would experience the love of a sister because even though I had been given three at my birth, I had never really experienced the true meaning of sisterhood outside of the relationship I had experienced early on with Faith and then again at our reunion.

I cannot help but to ponder the sheer miracle that Chinee has been in my life. How bittersweet the knowledge that the one person of whom I had literally fought to keep away from Chinee at the beginning of my life was given back to me by him at the end of his life. Faith and I finally met face to face when I arrived in Texas for Chinee's funeral; she had again driven the hundred miles to be my side. The meeting was overwhelmingly poignant and for me it was as though we had never separated. Only this time it was me who followed her lead.

I will never be able to repay the debt of gratitude I owe Faith. Her visit to Chinee's hospital room just days before his death brought the three of us full circle and re-established our relationship. We have remained in contact and have vowed never to allow time to separate us again. When we speak of Chinee, we speak of him as Sisters reliving sweeter moments in time when lived a demonstratively unselfish and caring person, our Brudda, Chinee.

By all that is holy, I can state that no portion of my life is occupied by regrets of the past. I still live my life following Papa's simplistic way of truth. Chinee was my keeper, thankfully so, and these 14 years later, he is as alive in my thoughts, memories, and heart as he ever was and will remain so as long as my own heart beats.

Rest easy Papa and Chinee, The Chickens have all gone to roost, all is well.

My Brother

CPSIA information can be obtained
at www.ICGtesting.com
Printed in the USA
BVHW071223220221
600770BV00004B/299